UNDERSTANDING BIBLICAL PROPHECY

A 30-DAY BIBLE STUDY

DR. DAVID JEREMIAH

Understanding Biblical Prophecy

Published by HarperChristian Resources, 3950 Sparks Drive SE, Suite 101, Grand Rapids, MI 49546, USA. HarperChristian Resources is a registered trademark of HarperCollins Christian Publishing, Inc.

Requests for information should be addressed to customercare@harpercollins.com.

ISBN 978-0-310-17511-7 (softcover)
ISBN 978-0-310-17512-4 (ebook)

HarperChristian Resources titles may be purchased in bulk for church, business, fundraising, or ministry use. For information, please e-mail ResourceSpecialist@ChurchSource.com.

HarperCollins Publishers, Macken House, 39/40 Mayor Street Upper, Dublin 1, D01 C9W8, Ireland (https://www.harpercollins.com).
Art direction: Ron Huizinga
Cover Design: © 2025 HarperCollins Christian Publishing
Interior Design: Inside Out Design

First Printing January 2026 / Printed in the United States of America

CONTENTS

INTRODUCTION

Would you like to know the future? I don't think I know anyone who would answer that question by saying "no." There would be many benefits to receiving insider information about tomorrow. We could identify opportunities before they arise and be ready to pounce on them. We could avoid catastrophes and failures—both our own and those of others. We could always be in the right place at the right time.

Just imagine the possibilities!

Unfortunately, our practical options for seeing into the future are limited at best. Weather forecasters have been especially unreliable throughout my lifetime. Fortune cookies and horoscopes are silliness and blasphemy and vagueness all wrapped together to form an ineffectual mess. So-called clairvoyants and others who claim to have a form of "second sight" are not only wrong most of the time, but they also consistently fail to capitalize on the kinds of opportunities I mentioned above.

The truth is that God alone has the power to see history like a piece of paper—past, present, and future all together in one display. He has that ability because He is the author of the past, the present, and the future. He is the Creator of time itself, which means He can look backward and forward with no difficulty and no hesitation.

Human beings, on the other hand, are not equipped to see the future—with one exception.

There have been times in history when God spoke to individuals about the future. These individuals are called prophets, and the words given to them by God are recorded in the Bible as prophecy. They are glimpses of what's to come. More, they are promises of what God will do.

Throughout the history of the church, the prophetic portions of Scripture have received an enormous amount of literary attention. Countless books claim to offer insight on the hundreds of topics related to biblical prophecy, all of them written from a wide variety of theological perspectives and positions on how to interpret Scripture. These studies can create a variety of questions, concerns, and even confusion in our minds. Sometimes it's difficult to see how obscure passages, distant places, and unfamiliar symbols can have any significance for our lives. After all, if we can't understand what the Bible is teaching, how in the world can it have any relevance to what we are experiencing today?

This drive to understand has been a major foundation of my ministry for decades—including the drive to understand and apply the truths communicated through biblical prophecy. My interest in that subject as a preacher and a writer has always been anchored in my love for the Bible, which I believe to be the inspired Word of God. I find it fascinating that the Bible dedicates more space to the subject of prophecy than almost any other. There are over eighteen hundred prophecies in God's Word concerning the first and second comings of Jesus Christ alone!

Obviously, prophecy is important to God, and He desires for us to understand His plans. He has given us His promises for a reason.

Sometimes biblical prophecy acts a warning, showing us the dangers ahead and encouraging us to go around them. Other times biblical prophecies are invitations. They draw us forward toward critical events on God's eschatological calendar—His plan for human history. Finally, there are other prophetic passages that are primarily informational. Meaning, they tell us important truths we need to know.

In these pages, we're going to explore thirty very specific, very important examples of biblical prophecy. Ten of those prophetic passages will be from the Old Testament, ten will be from the main portion of the New Testament, and ten will be from the book of Revelation, which has a special and specific focus on the end of our current age and beyond.

As we study these prophecies together, let's remember that doing so is more than an informational exercise. Much more! We're going to explore God's promises for humanity—God's promises for you and me. And we're going to see how those promises for tomorrow influence our daily lives today.

DAY 1

A GREAT NATION

"I will make you a great nation; I will bless you and make your name great; and you shall be a blessing. I will bless those who bless you, and I will curse him who curses you; and in you all the families of the earth shall be blessed."

GENESIS 12:2–3

CONTEXT

You may have noticed the early pages of the Bible move rather quickly. The first two chapters of Genesis describe God's creation of the universe, including the handcrafting of human beings. Then comes the Fall and the corruption of creation in Genesis 3. We get the first murder in human history in Genesis 4. Then, at the beginning of Genesis 6, we read a sentence that is as shocking as it is depressing: "The LORD saw that the wickedness of man was great in the earth, and that every intent of the thoughts of his heart was only evil continually" (verse 5).

Talk about everything going wrong in a hurry!

The pace doesn't slow down. Genesis 7–9 tells us about Noah, the ark, the great flood, and the aftermath. Genesis 10 quickly enumerates the nations that descended from Noah in a post-flood society. And Genesis 11 describes the strange story of the Tower of Babel.

It is not until Genesis 12 that the story really starts to slow down—and the reason is a man named Abram (later renamed Abraham by God). Specifically, the story slows down with an astonishing command that results in an amazing prophecy. Here's the command: "Now the LORD had said to Abram: 'Get out of your country, from your family and from your father's house, to a land that I will show you'" (verse 1).

Now, we tend to give credit to Abraham for the many ways in which he demonstrated his God-honoring faith later in life—and rightfully so. By faith, Abraham conquered kings and believed God's promise to make him the father of many nations, even though he and his wife, Sarah, were of advanced age and had no children. When Isaac finally did arrive on the scene, Abraham had enough faith to hold his son with open arms rather than turn him into an idol.

But I don't think we give Abraham enough credit for the courage he displayed in this first act of obedience. Look again at God's command. He told Abraham to leave his *country*, which at that time was a relatively advanced city called Ur of the Chaldeans. Not only that, but God told Abraham to leave his *family*—to leave his father's house, which would have included almost everyone and everything he valued. God commanded Abraham to travel far away to an entirely new place he had never seen and make a home there not just for himself but also for an entire nation. Plus, all this happened when Abraham was "seventy-five years old" (verse 4).

Amazingly, Abraham obeyed. Every word of God's command. He left what was familiar and went somewhere completely new simply because the Lord had told him to do so. As a result of that obedience, Abraham received a set of prophetic promises that have shaped not only biblical history but also *human history* for thousands of years.

Let's take a deeper look at those prophecies.

REFLECT

1. Read Genesis 12:1–9. What are the specific promises God made to Abraham in those verses?

2. What did God require of Abraham in order to receive those promises?

3. Verse 3 ends with a famous prophecy: "And in you all the families of the earth shall be blessed." That future blessing was made possible through Jesus, who was Abraham's descendant. What are some specific ways that prophecy has been fulfilled?

4. In verse 7, God told Abraham, "To your descendants I will give this land." He was referring to the land of Israel, once known as Canaan. How is that land, and God's promise connected to it, still relevant today?

APPLY

5. Beyond the physical land of Israel, God's promise to make Abraham into a "great nation" (the Jewish people) set the stage for the rest of the Old Testament, the rest of the New Testament, and everything we understand to be church history. What are some ways this prophecy has impacted your life?

6. Abraham risked a lot by choosing to leave his home and settle where God directed him. When has God asked you to take a step of faith that included genuine risk? How did you respond?

7. How do you typically respond when you feel God is leading you in a direction that is uncomfortable?

8. Abraham was willing to risk much because he trusted much. As a result, he experienced untold blessings. What are some obstacles that are currently hindering your ability to trust in God and His plans for your future?

AHEAD

The passage we've been exploring in Genesis 12:1–9 is what theologians refer to as a "conditional prophecy." Most of the time, when God declares that something will take place in the future, we can take that declaration to the bank. Prophecy will become reality simply because the Lord has declared it to be so.

However, there are other times when something must take place to trigger the fulfillment of prophecy. In this prophecy in Genesis 12, for example, each of the gifts that God said Abraham would receive was contingent on his obeying the initial command to "go from your country . . . to the land I will show you" (verse 1 NIV).

I mention this because you and I are not separated from biblical prophecy. We are not disconnected even from the major prophecies we'll be exploring in these pages. Instead, many of those prophecies have a direct application to both our present and our future. Indeed, many of God's prophetic promises will be fulfilled even through our lives and our choices each day.

"Get out of your country, from your family and from your father's house, to a land that I will show you."

GENESIS 12:1

When Abraham heard that command, he obeyed that command. As a result, he received a set of prophetic promises that have since shaped human history.

DAY 2

AN ETERNAL THRONE

*"When your days are fulfilled and you rest with your fathers,
I will set up your seed after you, who will come from your body,
and I will establish his kingdom. He shall build a house for
My name, and I will establish the throne of his kingdom forever.
I will be his Father, and he shall be My son."*

2 SAMUEL 7:12–14

CONTEXT

David walked a long road before being crowned king of Israel. Yes, he was a young man when Samuel anointed him as the future king of God's chosen people. But Saul was still the present king, and he had no plans to relinquish the throne willingly. As David became more popular after defeating Goliath, Saul became more jealous. Eventually he determined to kill David, and he spent several years chasing the younger man throughout the wilderness.

Fifteen years after David's anointing, Saul and his sons were killed during a battle against the Philistines. That opened the door for David to be crowned king of the territory inhabited by the tribe of Judah—but not all of Israel. It took another seven years for the other tribes to finally recognize David as their king (2 Samuel 5:1–5).

During David's time in the wilderness, he was forced to live in caves and other less-than-luxurious accommodations. That may be one of the reasons why David chose to commission a royal palace in Jerusalem near the end of his reign as king. David oversaw the construction of this palace of cedar—but soon after felt a twang of conscience. The king had a palace, but God still dwelt in a tent outside the city.

Moving swiftly, David consulted with the prophet Nathan about building a more permanent home for God's name to dwell—a glorious temple. Yet God responded in a surprising way. Through that same prophet, He rejected David's plan to build a temple. Instead, He made two critical promises that He would accomplish Himself. First, God promised to "plant" His people in the land of Israel as a place of safety and peace (2 Samuel 7:10–11). Second, He promised to establish a "house" for David that went well beyond walls of cedar.

Here is the core of that promise:

> "When your days are fulfilled and you rest with your fathers, I will set up your seed after you, who will come from your body, and I will establish his kingdom. He shall build a house for My name, and I will establish the throne of his kingdom forever. I will be his Father, and he shall be My son. If he commits iniquity, I will chasten him with the rod of men and with the blows of the sons of men. But My mercy shall not depart from him, as I took it from Saul, whom I removed from before you. And your house and your kingdom shall be established forever before you. Your throne shall be established forever" (verses 12–16).

These prophetic promises are significant hinges on which human history bends and turns. They point forward to the importance of Israel on the world stage and the central role of the Messiah in our past, present, and future. Let's take a deeper look to learn more.

REFLECT

1. Read through 2 Samuel 7:1–17 to get the full picture of these important prophecies. What can we learn from these verses about David? What can we learn about God?

2. What promises did God make in that passage? List as many as you can find.

3. Biblical prophecies often include several layers of meaning. Look again at verses 12–16. Which of the promises in those verses apply to David's son Solomon? Which promises apply to the Messiah, who would be one of David's descendants?

4. Read Luke 1:30–33 to see Gabriel's announcement to Mary about the incarnation of Jesus. Where do you see specific connections between those verses and the covenant established in 2 Samuel 7?

APPLY

5. God made clear in His promises to David that Jesus would sit on the throne of David "forever." How does the eternal nature of that promise apply to you in the present? How does it apply to your future?

6. Jesus is the fulfillment of God's prophecy to David, which means He is King. On an emotional level, how do you respond to the idea of having a King and being part of a kingdom?

7. On a practical level, what does it mean for you to recognize Jesus as King not just of the world or the universe—but of your life specifically?

8. What are some practical steps you can take in the near future to actively submit to Jesus as your King?

AHEAD

In 2 Samuel 7, David began by expressing his desire to build a temple for God as an act of worship (verses 1–2). God turned the tables by denying David's request and making several promises of His own. Specifically, the Davidic covenant established in that chapter includes God's promise to:

- Plant the people of Israel in the promised land as an eternal inheritance (verse 10).
- Protect the Israelites from their enemies (verse 10).
- Provide a way for David's lineage to continue forever through the coming of the Messiah (verse 12).
- Provide a way for David's rule (his throne) to continue as well (verse 16).

As you might imagine, David was overwhelmed by the generosity of these incredible promises. He declared, "Now, O LORD God, the word which You have spoken concerning Your servant and concerning his house, establish it forever and do as You have said. So let Your name be magnified forever, saying, 'The LORD of hosts is the God over Israel.' And let the house of Your servant David be established before You. For You, O LORD of hosts, God of Israel, have revealed this to Your servant, saying, 'I will build you a house.' Therefore Your servant has found it in his heart to pray this prayer to You" (verses 25–27).

David accepted God's gifts with gratitude, with thanksgiving, and with praise. May we always do the same.

"I will set up your seed after you, who will come from your body, and I will establish his kingdom."

2 SAMUEL 7:12

The prophetic promises God made to David are significant hinges on which human history bends and turns.

DAY 3

A CHILD IS BORN

For unto us a Child is born,
Unto us a Son is given;
And the government will be upon His shoulder.
And His name will be called
Wonderful, Counselor, Mighty God,
Everlasting Father, Prince of Peace.

ISAIAH 9:6

CONTEXT

Here is one of the most important principles we can learn when studying Scripture: Biblical prophecy often contains layers. What I mean is that prophetic passages are usually packed with several different layers of meaning and/or application.

The Messianic prophecies of Isaiah offer a good example of this layering effect. One of the most famous of those prophecies (especially around the Christmas season) can be found in Isaiah 7:

> "Therefore the Lord Himself will give you a sign: Behold, the virgin shall conceive and bear a Son, and shall call His name Immanuel. Curds and honey He shall eat, that He may know to refuse the evil and choose the good. For before the Child shall know to refuse the evil and choose the good, the land that you dread will be forsaken by both her kings. The LORD will bring the king of Assyria upon you and your people and your father's house—days that have not come since the day that Ephraim departed from Judah" (verses 14–17).

First, we need to check the immediate context of this passage. In Isaiah 7, the prophet was speaking to King Ahaz of Judah. At the time, the people of Judah were under threat from the armies of Syria and Israel (described as "Ephraim" throughout the chapter). Isaiah encouraged Ahaz to ask God for a sign of coming salvation, but Ahaz refused—apparently in an attempt to be seen as humble.

Frustrated, Isaiah declared that God Himself would provide a sign for Judah's salvation in the form of Isaiah's own son (8:3). Before that son was old enough "to refuse the evil and choose the good" (7:15), the might of Assyria would attack and destroy Judah's enemies, bringing salvation to God's people.

So, that's the first layer of the prophecy. But not the only layer. God's promise spoken through Isaiah also pointed forward to a much more important form of salvation—a spiritual rescue from sin that would be secured when a literal "virgin" conceived and bore a son. That prophecy was fulfilled through the birth of Jesus Christ, who is "Immanuel," God with us.

As we'll see, this same principle applies to several key prophetic passages throughout the book of Isaiah, including today's key text in chapter 9. That entire chapter is packed with promises pertaining to the Messiah. Isaiah starts by describing a people walking in darkness who would see a "great light" (9:2). It ends with a forceful declaration of God's wrath and judgment against sin. In the middle is a series of promises that brought joy to the people of Isaiah's day—promises that still bring joy to followers of Jesus in our own day.

Let's explore those promises together.

REFLECT

1. Read Isaiah 9:6–7. Which of those promises were fulfilled during the life and ministry of Jesus? Which of those promises have yet to be fulfilled?

2. Both in ancient times and today, you can learn a lot about a person by the titles he or she receives. What do we learn about Jesus from the names and titles listed in verse 6?

3. Jesus is the King of kings, and He offers the standard for justice throughout heaven and earth. What are some of the ways Jesus has already established justice for His people? Where do you still see injustice in our world that needs to be corrected?

4. Read Isaiah 35:5–7 to see another example of Messianic prophecy. Where do you see connections between those verses and Jesus' ministry as recorded in the Gospels?

APPLY

5. The reality of layers within biblical prophecy is both exciting and potentially confusing. How should the existence of those layers influence the way we study God's Word?

6. How should the layered nature of biblical prophecy influence the way we apply prophetic passages to our present and our future?

7. King Jesus will establish His kingdom with "justice." Where do you see injustice currently taking place in your community?

8. Where do you have an opportunity right now to take a stand for justice, whether locally or around the world?

AHEAD

Here's a question you may be thinking after exploring Isaiah 9 more deeply: If the prophecies in verses 6–7 have not yet been fulfilled completely, when will that fulfillment occur? In other words, when will Jesus officially take the government of our world onto His shoulders? When will Jesus reclaim the throne of His ancestor David? When will He fully establish justice and peace forever?

The answer that may come to mind is "heaven," and there's some truth to that response. Jesus is already reigning in heaven as King of the universe, and that reign will never end. Similarly, heaven is a place of perfect justice, perfect peace, and perfect joy.

Yet what about the promise that Jesus will reclaim the throne of David? That promise will come true! Specifically, Jesus will return to our world as King, not only of heaven, but also of earth. He will sit on the throne of David in the city of Jerusalem during the thousand-year period of time often described as the Millennium. We'll learn more about that future kingdom as we move through these pages, for many biblical prophecies point forward to that glorious reign.

For now, remember that God's plans for this world are still in process. His promises are still coming true. And the end result of His plan will be an eternal kingdom filled with goodness and justice and peace and joy for all of eternity.

"Behold, the virgin shall conceive and bear a Son,
and shall call His name Immanuel."

ISAIAH 7:14

God's promise, spoken through Isaiah, points to a spiritual rescue from sin that would be secured when a literal "virgin" conceived and bore a son.

DAY 4

BY HIS STRIPES WE ARE HEALED

But He was wounded for our transgressions,
He was bruised for our iniquities;
The chastisement for our peace was upon Him,
And by His stripes we are healed.
All we like sheep have gone astray;
We have turned, every one, to his own way;
And the LORD has laid on Him the iniquity of us all.

ISAIAH 53:5–6

CONTEXT

The prophet Isaiah ministered to four separate kings in Jerusalem from approximately 739 to 686 BC—a span of more than fifty years. It makes sense, then, that the book bearing Isaiah's name includes some of the most significant prophecies in the Old Testament. As we've already seen, several of those prophecies pointed forward to the birth of the Messiah, which took place almost seven hundred years after Isaiah's death. But Isaiah also prophesied about the Messiah's life and public ministry. And His crucifixion.

Specifically, the book of Isaiah contains four poetic passages that scholars often refer to as "Servant Songs" because they point forward to the ministry of the Messiah as God's divine Servant. The first of these songs is found in Isaiah 42:1–9, and it declares the Messiah's focus on restoring justice across the earth. The second song comes in 49:1–13 and describes the Messiah's mission of salvation. The third song is found in 50:4–11, which speaks of the Messiah's obedience to the Father even in the midst of persecution.

The fourth Servant Song is the longest. It officially begins in Isaiah 52:13 and continues through 53:12. This is the most famous of the four songs because it predicts, in startling and even graphic detail, the willing sacrifice of Jesus on the cross. For example: "He is despised and rejected by men, a Man of sorrows and acquainted with grief. And we hid, as it were, our faces from Him; He was despised, and we did not esteem Him" (53:3).

The level of detail really is startling. According to Isaiah, the Messiah:

- Would have his face marred so badly that people would be astonished to see it (52:14).
- Would be raised in lowly conditions with nothing special about His lineage (53:2).
- Would be despised and rejected by men (53:3).
- Would be wounded in a way that produced "stripes" (53:5).
- Would spend time as a prisoner (53:8).
- Would be buried in the grave of someone who is "rich" (53:9).
- Would be "numbered with the transgressors"—lumped in with the other criminals of His day (53:12).

Remember, each of these biblical prophecies was written seven hundred years before Jesus launched His public ministry or set foot in Jerusalem. They offer proof that God is sovereign over the past, present, and future. They also offer proof that Jesus alone is the Messiah about which so many prophecies were written throughout the Old Testament. They are a powerful proof of the truth of God's Word.

I hope you'll be open to the wonder of that truth as we further explore these passages.

REFLECT

1. Isaiah's fourth "Servant Song" begins with 52:13–15. What did the prophet communicate about the future Messiah in those verses?

2. Make it a point to read Isaiah 53:1–12 out loud. As you do so, write down the specific connections you notice between Isaiah's prophecy and Jesus' life, ministry, and death. Which of those connections feel most important to you? Why?

3. It's a mistake to think that we can learn about Jesus only through the Gospels of the New Testament. The reality is all Scripture is focused on Christ. What can we learn about Jesus' nature, character, and mission from Isaiah 53?

4. The timing of Isaiah's prophecy is critical. Even secular scholars don't dispute that Isaiah wrote his book long before Jesus' life and crucifixion. Given that reality, how does this passage expand your understanding of the nature and purpose of biblical prophecy?

APPLY

5. Which elements of Isaiah 52 and 53 seem most important when it comes to proving the reliability and truthfulness of God's Word? Why?

6. Isaiah 53 in particular paints a vivid picture of Jesus' crucifixion—His death by torture on the cross. What emotions do you experience when you read that chapter? Why?

7. What are some ways you can express gratitude and thankfulness for Jesus' sacrifice on your behalf?

8. Isaiah 53:5 declares that we are "healed" through the stripes Jesus endured on His way to the cross. Where do you need to experience that healing in your life right now?

AHEAD

If you've spent much time in the church, you've likely come across the idea that God functions one way in the Old Testament and a totally different way in the New Testament. According to this way of thinking, God primarily operates out of wrath and judgment in His dealings with people in the Old Testament but switches to become more focused on love and grace throughout the New Testament.

This division of God's nature and character is a mistake. At best, it's a well-meaning misconception. At worst, it is an effort to twist reality (and affect our theology) by ignoring the teaching of Scripture.

Isaiah 53 offers excellent proof that God's nature does not change. That's because this chapter offers some of the most loving and love-saturated passages in all of Scripture. Consider verse 5: "But He was wounded for our transgressions, He was bruised for our iniquities; the chastisement for our peace was upon Him, and by His stripes we are healed."

What a wonderful distillation of the gospel found smack in the middle of the Old Testament! What a testament to God's unfailing love!

He is despised and rejected by men,
a Man of sorrows and acquainted with grief.

ISAIAH 53:3

Biblical prophecy reveals that God is sovereign
over the past, the present, and the future—and offers
astounding proof that Jesus alone is the Messiah.

DAY 5

A NEW COVENANT

"Behold, the days are coming, says the LORD, when I will make a new covenant with the house of Israel and with the house of Judah. . . . This is the covenant that I will make with the house of Israel after those days, says the LORD: I will put My law in their minds, and write it on their hearts; and I will be their God, and they shall be My people. No more shall every man teach his neighbor, and every man his brother, saying, 'Know the LORD,' for they all shall know Me, from the least of them to the greatest of them, says the LORD. For I will forgive their iniquity, and their sin I will remember no more."

JEREMIAH 31:31, 33–34

CONTEXT

One thing that becomes abundantly clear whenever we read through the Bible is that God is a fan of covenants. At several stages of biblical history, God made a concerted effort to establish a covenant with His people and then to deal with those people according to the provisions of those covenants.

This process goes all the way back to the beginning with Adam and Eve: "Then the LORD God took the man and put him in the garden of Eden to tend and keep it. And the LORD God commanded the man, saying, 'Of every tree of the garden you may freely eat; but of the tree of the knowledge of good and evil you shall not eat, for in the day that you eat of it you shall surely die'" (Genesis 2:15–17).

This covenant was relatively simple: God established Adam and Eve (and their descendants) as stewards of Eden, and by extension stewards of all the earth. That was an incredible blessing, and it came with a single prohibition: not to eat from the Tree of Knowledge of Good and Evil. We all know how that turned out, unfortunately.

God's second covenant was with Noah. After the flood, God once again commanded humanity to be fruitful and multiply as stewards over the earth. This time, God also promised never to flood the earth again, offering the rainbow as a "sign" of that covenant (Genesis 9).

Next came God's covenant with Abraham, which we started exploring back on Day 1. That covenant included multiple provisions, but most prominent was God's promise to turn Abraham's descendants into a great nation, to bless them, and to one day bring them to a land of their own—a land that they could always call home. The "signing" of that covenant is described in Genesis 15.

The most famous covenant in the Old Testament is the one God established with Moses and the Israelites on Mount Sinai—what we often call the Mosaic covenant. According to this agreement, if the Israelites followed God's law, including the Ten Commandments, they would receive God's favor, blessing, and long life in the promised land. If they rebelled against God's law, they would experience sorrow and poverty, and be removed from the land. Over centuries, God's people continued to choose the latter path.

Again, what's notable here is that God prefers to engage with people based on covenants. That's why these words from the book of Jeremiah are so important: "Behold, the days are coming, says the LORD, when I will make *a new covenant* with the house of Israel and with the house of Judah" (Jeremiah 31:31, emphasis added).

Let's explore that new covenant, including some of the ways its provisions impact us today.

REFLECT

1. Read again through the different Old Testament covenants listed above. What did God offer to do or provide in each of those covenants? What did He require His people to do or provide?

2. Read Jeremiah 31:31–34 out loud. Importantly, this new covenant would be made "with the house of Israel and with the house of Judah," although the church has also been incorporated into that covenant through the work of Jesus. Why is it noteworthy that God included the Jewish people in this new covenant?

3. What are the provisions of this new covenant? What did God promise to do or provide, and what does He require of those who participate in that covenant?

4. We can read about the official establishment of this new covenant in Matthew 26:26–29. How do those verses connect with the description of the new covenant from Jeremiah 31? How does that description connect with the broader life and ministry of Jesus?

APPLY

5. The new covenant prophesied by Jeremiah isn't an academic principle or a relic from centuries past. It is active right now. What are some specific ways that covenant applies directly to your life?

6. What are some additional covenants (or contracts) that are important in your life? What steps do you take to show you are serious about honoring those contracts?

7. What are some possible steps you can take as a disciple of Jesus to show that you are serious about honoring the "new covenant" He offered through His death and resurrection?

8. One provision of this new covenant is that we will "know the LORD" (Jeremiah 31:34). How satisfied do you feel right now in your relationship with God? Meaning, how satisfied do you feel in terms of knowing God and being known by Him?

AHEAD

Prophecy has layers, as we've seen, and that is the case with Jeremiah's prophetic passage announcing the "new covenant" between God and humanity. It's easy to believe that prophecy has already been fulfilled completely—that Jesus' death and resurrection have opened the door for God's law to be written on our hearts, for our sins to be forgiven, and for each of us from the least to the greatest to know God in a personal way.

All of that is true at this moment. But does that mean the prophecy has been completely fulfilled? No.

Remember that Jeremiah was speaking to "the house of Israel" and "the house of Judah." God said, "But this is the covenant that I will make with the house of Israel after those days," which means Jeremiah's prophecy will not be complete until the Jewish people return to God and recognize Jesus as their Messiah. That moment won't occur until the Tribulation, when the hate and cruelty of the Antichrist drives God's chosen people back to Him.

Until then, as the church, we can celebrate our inclusion in this new covenant. And we can pray for the final redemption of all of God's people.

"Behold, the days are coming . . . when I will make a new covenant with the house of Israel and with the house of Judah."

JEREMIAH 31:31

We, the church, can celebrate our inclusion in this new covenant—and we can pray for the final redemption of all God's people when they recognize Jesus as their Messiah.

DAY 6

DRY BONES LIVE

Again He said to me, "Prophesy to these bones, and say to them, 'O dry bones, hear the word of the Lord*! Thus says the Lord* God *to these bones: "Surely I will cause breath to enter into you, and you shall live. I will put sinews on you and bring flesh upon you, cover you with skin and put breath in you; and you shall live. Then you shall know that I am the* Lord*."'"*

EZEKIEL 37:4–6

CONTEXT

Ezekiel was twenty-five years old when the armies of Babylon surrounded Jerusalem in 597 BC. Those armies did not destroy Jerusalem—not yet. But they did take ten thousand captives from among the youngest and most educated members of Jewish society. This was a common tactic used by empires in the ancient world, designed to ensure that a potentially rebellious nation would choose to behave itself rather than risk harm to the captives. Meanwhile, those captives were incorporated into Babylonian society, which strengthened the empire.

Five years after Ezekiel's captivity, God called Ezekiel to serve as a prophet. Unfortunately, the job description was less than encouraging: "Son of man, I am sending you to the children of Israel, to a rebellious nation that has rebelled against Me; they and their fathers have transgressed against Me to this very day. For they are impudent and stubborn children. I am sending you to them, and you shall say to them, 'Thus says the Lord God'" (Ezekiel 2:3–4).

God called Ezekiel to deliver many messages to the Jewish captives living in Babylon, and most of them were bad news. Ezekiel declared that the armies of Babylon would again surround Jerusalem and lay siege to the Holy City. Worse, that siege would result in the destruction of both Jerusalem and the temple.

For years, Ezekiel pleaded with the Jewish people, both in Babylon and those still in Jerusalem, to repent of their idolatry and return to the Lord. But for years the people refused to listen. They believed God would never allow His favorite city to be destroyed—and certainly not the temple where His name dwelt. So they continued living as they had always lived, ignoring the warnings of God. Of course, the Babylonians did eventually lay siege to Jerusalem. Then they destroyed it, along with the temple. God's word spoken through Ezekiel came true.

Then something incredible happened. In that moment of deep despair, God gave Ezekiel a vision of Israel's future—a vision that radiated with hope. It started with a vision of a valley filled with dry bones, which represented the nation of Israel. As Ezekiel watched, the bones began to stir, then knit themselves together with sinew and flesh until a great multitude of people filled the valley. The dry bones lived! As God later explained, those bones represented the house of Israel, which was currently in ruins but would one day be restored.

Later, Ezekiel received a similar vision in which God commanded him to take two sticks and connect them with his hands to form a single, unified branch. That image represented the two kingdoms of God's people—Israel in the north and Judah in the south—which would be reunified at a future point. In short, during one of the darkest seasons of Israel's history—when many of God's chosen people were convinced Israel had no more history—the Lord stepped in to offer the light of hope for the future. Let's explore that hope in greater detail.

REFLECT

1. Read the full picture of Ezekiel's vision of the dry bones in 37:1–14. What specific promises did God make to Israel within that prophecy?

2. Given the context, there's no question that this vision primarily speaks to the eventual restoration of the Jewish nation. But in what ways does this vision provide a preview of the gospel message? Of the doctrine we call salvation?

3. Look also at Ezekiel's vision of the two sticks in 37:15–28. How would you summarize or describe the primary message of that vision?

4. What specific promises did God make in verses 15–28? Which of those promises have already come true, and which have not?

APPLY

5. The relationship between the Jewish people and the church has been complicated ever since the launch of the church almost two thousand years ago. What are some words you would use to describe that relationship today?

6. The process of salvation is often described as bringing spiritual life to a person who was spiritually dead. What are some of the ways this "new life" has impacted your past and your present?

7. Verses 15–28 describe the unification of Israel's two houses, which were often in conflict throughout the Old Testament. How have you experienced conflict or disagreements among Christians in your community?

8. Where do you have opportunities to be a peacemaker in those conflicts?

AHEAD

Ezekiel 37 presents two visions, both of which point forward to a moment of restoration for God's people. Interestingly, both of those visions have a strong connection to the physical land of Israel.

In the vision of the dry bones, God promised, "I will put My Spirit in you, and you shall live, and I will place you in your own land" (verse 14). In the vision of the two sticks, He added, "Surely I will take the children of Israel from among the nations, wherever they have gone, and will gather them from every side and bring them into their own land; and I will make them one nation in the land, on the mountains of Israel; and one king shall be king over them all; they shall no longer be two nations, nor shall they ever be divided into two kingdoms again" (verses 21–22).

These visions have always been significant, both to the children of Israel and to the church. But they became even more significant on May 14, 1948. That's when Israel was restored as a nation after World War II. Since that time, millions of Jews have left the nations in which they were scattered and returned to the promised land—just as God promised.

Once again, these events place an exclamation point on God's sovereign power over all things, including the ins and outs of human history. We can be sure that whatever He says will happen—will happen!

"O My people, I will open your graves and cause you to come up from your graves, and bring you into the land of Israel."

EZEKIEL 37:12

During one of the darkest seasons of Israel's history, the Lord stepped in to offer His people the light of hope for the future.

DAY 7

THE RISE AND FALL OF KINGDOMS

Daniel answered in the presence of the king, and said, "The secret which the king has demanded, the wise men, the astrologers, the magicians, and the soothsayers cannot declare to the king. But there is a God in heaven who reveals secrets, and He has made known to King Nebuchadnezzar what will be in the latter days."

DANIEL 2:27–28

CONTEXT

Daniel lived and ministered at a critical juncture in biblical history. Born around 620 BC, he was one of the talented young men taken captive by the Babylonians when they began their conquest of Judah and Jerusalem. He was brought back to Babylon and educated to become a useful servant in the governmental machinery of that kingdom.

One reason why this was such a critical moment in history is that God was in the process of transferring power in the ancient Middle East from the Jews to the Gentiles. Much of the Old Testament describes not only the creation and growth of humanity as a whole but also the foundation of the Jewish people through Abraham—and later the foundation of the Jewish nation within the promised land of Canaan. Through figures including Saul, David, and Solomon, God established Israel as a powerhouse in the region.

Because of Israel's disobedience, however, their power and influenced waned. In fact, the nation of Israel functionally came to an end when Jerusalem was destroyed by the Babylonians in 586 BC. From that moment forward, Gentiles became the ruling force in that region. That remained the case during the time of Jesus, throughout the launch and growth of the church, and all the way up until the nation of Israel was restored in 1948.

Daniel, though an official in the court of King Nebuchadnezzar, also remained a prophet of the Most High God. One of the most striking moments of Daniel's prophetic ministry came when he both described and interpreted a vision given to Nebuchadnezzar by God:

> "You, O king, were watching; and behold, a great image! . . . This image's head was of fine gold, its chest and arms of silver, its belly and thighs of bronze, its legs of iron, its feet partly of iron and partly of clay. You watched while a stone was cut out without hands, which struck the image on its feet of iron and clay, and broke them in pieces. Then the iron, the clay, the bronze, the silver, and the gold were crushed together, and became like chaff from the summer threshing floors; the wind carried them away so that no trace of them was found. And the stone that struck the image became a great mountain and filled the whole earth" (Daniel 2:31–35).

The four sections of the statue predicted the four major empires that would rule the promised land and its surrounding regions from the time of Daniel up to the time of Christ: (1) the head of gold represented Babylon; (2) the chest and arms of silver represented the alliance of the Medes and Persians, which conquered Babylon during the reign of Belshazzar; (3) the belly and thighs of bronze represented the Greek Empire under the rule of Alexander the Great; and (4) the legs and feet made of iron and clay represented the Roman Empire.

REFLECT

1. Read Daniel 2:27–45 to see the whole scope of Daniel's message to King Nebuchadnezzar, his description of the dream, and his interpretation of that dream. What strikes you as most interesting or relevant from this prophetic passage?

2. Read Daniel's interpretation of the king's dream in verses 36–45. What specific events did Daniel predict in those verses? What specific promises did he make, not only to King Nebuchadnezzar, but also to future readers of this prophecy?

3. Later in his life, Daniel himself received a prophetic vision that highlighted key aspects of the future. Read that vision in Daniel 7:1–14. Then read the interpretation of that vision in 7:15–27. Where do you see connections between Nebuchadnezzar's dream and Daniel's vision?

4. Look specifically at Daniel's vision of the "Ancient of Days" in 7:9-14. What can we learn from these verses about God's nature and character? What can we learn about Jesus?

APPLY

5. God spoke to both Nebuchadnezzar and Daniel in ways that revealed God's detailed understanding of the future. These interactions are critical proofs of God's sovereignty. What does that reality mean for your life, specifically?

6. How does the reality of God's sovereignty influence your actions and attitudes in the present? How does it influence your dreams and plans for the future?

7. Daniel was a leader in Babylonian society and also a child of God. The same dual citizenship applies to Christians today. In what ways have you felt tension between the values of your country and the values of God's kingdom?

8. What are some steps you can take to align yourself with the values and priorities of God's kingdom over and above the values and priorities of modern culture?

AHEAD

As a reminder, the colossal statue in Nebuchadnezzar's dream represented the four primary kingdoms that would rule over the known world from Daniel's day until the time of Christ. These were the empires of Babylon, Medo-Persia, Greece, and Rome. Yet the king's dream also highlighted a separate empire—or we might call it a kingdom—in the form of a great stone that struck the statue and destroyed it. Afterward, "the stone that struck the image became a great mountain and filled the whole earth" (Daniel 2:35).

Here's what Daniel had to say about that kingdom in his interpretation to Nebuchadnezzar: "And in the days of these kings the God of heaven will set up a kingdom which shall never be destroyed; and the kingdom shall not be left to other people; it shall break in pieces and consume all these kingdoms, and it shall stand forever" (verse 44).

Daniel was speaking, of course, about the kingdom of God. That kingdom was established on earth through the birth, life, death, and resurrection of Jesus Christ. That kingdom remains on earth today through the work of its citizens, who make up the church.

That kingdom has not yet "filled the whole earth," as Daniel described. Yet as certainly as Daniel's prophecies about the four empires came true, so will his prophecy about God's heavenly kingdom. One day, Jesus will reign from Jerusalem as the true King of kings, and His dominion will spread over all the earth. May that day come soon!

"The God of heaven will set up a kingdom which shall never be destroyed . . . it shall break in pieces and consume all these kingdoms, and it shall stand forever."

DANIEL 2:44

Daniel was speaking about the kingdom of God. One day, Jesus will reign from Jerusalem as the true King of kings, and His dominion will spread over all the earth.

DAY 8

THE SEVENTY WEEKS

"Seventy weeks are determined
For your people and for your holy city,
To finish the transgression,
To make an end of sins,
To make reconciliation for iniquity,
To bring in everlasting righteousness,
To seal up vision and prophecy,
And to anoint the Most Holy."

DANIEL 9:24

CONTEXT

The prophet Daniel was near the end of his life—probably eighty-five or eighty-six years old—when he received one of the most important prophecies not only of his life but in all of Scripture. By this point, Daniel had been in Babylon for six or seven *decades*. He had witnessed the fall of Babylon as a nation at the hands of the Medes and Persians, and he had become a key advisor for the new king, whose name was Darius. (It was Darius, you might remember, whom the other officials tricked into throwing Daniel in the lions' den.)

Decades before, Daniel had interpreted King Nebuchadnezzar's dream of an enormous statue as a prophecy for the rise and fall of four empires over hundreds of years. Now, through a conversation with the angel Gabriel, Daniel received a prophecy so comprehensive it included both the triumphal entry of Jesus into Jerusalem and the seven years of the Tribulation at the end of our current age.

It all started with prayer. Daniel was immersed in "speaking, praying, and confessing" (9:20) when he received another visit from the angel Gabriel. The angel declared that "seventy weeks are determined" for the nation of Israel as part of God's plan for history. Each of those "weeks" represents a period not of seven days but of seven years.

Now, here's where things get really interesting. Gabriel declared, "Know therefore and understand, that from the going forth of the command to restore and build Jerusalem until Messiah the Prince, there shall be seven weeks and sixty-two weeks" (9:25). The first "seven weeks" describe the time required for Israel to rebuild the temple, and the remaining "sixty-two weeks" laid out how long it would take for the Messiah to appear.

We know from the book of Nehemiah that King Artaxerxes issued a proclamation to rebuild Jerusalem on March 14, 445 BC. Several scholars have done wonderful work mapping out the sixty-nine "weeks" of years (the "seven weeks and sixty-two weeks" described in verse 25), which comes out to 173,880 days.

Do you know what date occurs 173,880 days after March 14, 445 BC? The answer is April 6, AD 32. Do you know what event occurred on April 6, AD 32? The answer is the triumphal entry. Jesus presented Himself to Jerusalem *on the exact day* prophesied by the angel Gabriel.

Once again, I love God's Word! I love the wonder of biblical prophecy!

Now, you might be thinking, *Daniel described seventy weeks, so why did everything stop at sixty-nine weeks?* Well, nothing stopped. But there was a divine pause. When the Jewish people rejected Jesus as their Messiah, God paused His plan for prophetic history and pivoted to something new: the church. That seventieth week will come into play, and we will discuss it later. But for now, let's take a closer look at Daniel 9:20–27.

REFLECT

1. Read Daniel 9:20–27 to get the biblical context for Daniel's "seventy weeks" prophecy. What questions come to mind when you read those verses? What seems confusing or especially interesting?

2. Gabriel identified six separate purposes "for your people and for your holy city" (verse 24) connected with the prophetic period of seventy weeks. What are those six purposes? Which of those have already been fulfilled or partially realized?

3. As mentioned above, Gabriel predicted the exact day when the Messiah would enter Jerusalem and present Himself as God's Anointed One. Read about that moment in Luke 19:28–44. Where do you see evidence in those verses that Jesus knowingly fulfilled the prophecies included in Daniel 9?

4. There are some elements of Daniel's "seventy weeks" prophecy that have yet to be fulfilled—specifically in verse 27. How would you summarize the primary message of that verse? What is it describing?

APPLY

5. One key element of biblical prophecy is that God is supernatural—meaning, something that can't be explained by natural or logical means. How do you respond to this supernatural element of Scripture? How do you feel about it?

6. When have you been in a situation where you felt the need to defend or explain the accuracy of Scripture to someone who was skeptical? How did you respond?

7. To what degree are you interested in and/or excited about trying to determine what the Bible says about the future? What are some benefits of studying Scripture in that way?

8. What are some potential risks or dangers of attempting to "see the future" based on the prophecies in Daniel and in the rest of God's Word?

AHEAD

You may have heard people claim there is no direct evidence for the truth or reliability of the Bible. You may even have heard such claims coming from Christians who say the Bible must be taken by "faith" rather than "facts." However, such claims are not based in reality, nor are they helpful.

The Bible is supernatural, but it also presents us with a great deal of evidence in support of the doctrine we call inspiration—the idea that the words and the promises and the insights of Scripture come directly from God Himself. To state it plainly, there are plenty of reasons to believe the Bible is a gift to humanity from God, and there are plenty of reasons to trust that what we find in the Bible is true.

Daniel 9 is a wonderful example. We know from historical analysis that Daniel was born more than six hundred years before Jesus. We know that Daniel wrote the words to his prophetic book long before the alliance of the Medes and Persians, long before Alexander the Great, long before the Romans entered the scene, and long before Jesus asked two of His disciples to bring Him a colt on the day of the triumphal entry.

Yet in all of those cases, Daniel predicted historical events with stunning accuracy. When we understand the precision of biblical prophecy, we can know without a shadow of a doubt that God's Word is true.

"Seventy weeks are determined for your people and for your holy city, to finish the transgression, to make an end of sins."

DANIEL 9:24

When the Jewish people rejected Jesus as their Messiah, God paused His plan for prophetic history and pivoted to something new: the church—but the seventieth week will *come into play.*

DAY 9

THE SEVENTIETH WEEK

"At that time Michael shall stand up,
The great prince who stands watch over the sons of your people;
And there shall be a time of trouble,
Such as never was since there was a nation,
Even to that time.
And at that time your people shall be delivered,
Every one who is found written in the book."

DANIEL 12:1

CONTEXT

The book of Daniel contains several prophetic visions that reach forward to describe the future. Some of those visions describe events that took place decades or centuries after Daniel's time. Other visions describe events that still remain unfulfilled in our time—with the Tribulation being most notable among them.

As we saw in the material for Day 8, the angel Gabriel declared that "seventy weeks" had been set aside in God's prophetic calendar during which God would deal with Israel in a number of ways. Those seventy weeks are best understood as seventy "sevens" of years, or 490 total years, beginning with the proclamation from King Artaxerxes to rebuild the temple in Jerusalem. The angel said there would be sixty-nine total "weeks" (483 years) between that proclamation and the arrival of the Messiah in Jerusalem. Sure enough, the triumphal entry of Jesus took place 483 years later.

But what about that seventieth week? As we saw previously, God pressed pause on His prophetic calendar when the Jewish people as a whole rejected Jesus as their Messiah. He launched the church instead, and He has used the church to spread the gospel from that point until the end of this age.

When this age comes to an end, however, our world will experience the final week of Gabriel's prophecy—the final seven years. We often refer to those years as the Tribulation.

Look again at Gabriel's words from Daniel 9: "He will confirm a covenant with many for one 'seven.' In the middle of the 'seven' he will put an end to sacrifice and offering. And at the temple he will set up an abomination that causes desolation, until the end that is decreed is poured out on him" (verse 27 NIV).

The "he" in that verse is the Antichrist. At the beginning of the Tribulation, the Antichrist will establish a peace treaty with Israel for seven years. Halfway through, he will break that treaty and viciously attack the promised land, including Jerusalem. The final three and a half years of the Tribulation will be chaos and terror and violence unlike anything we've ever seen.

In the words of the angel from Daniel 12, "And there shall be a time of trouble, such as never was since there was a nation, even to that time" (verse 1). And in the words of Jesus, "For then there will be great tribulation, such as has not been since the beginning of the world until this time, no, nor ever shall be. And unless those days were shortened, no flesh would be saved" (Matthew 24:21–22).

We're going explore the Tribulation more broadly near the end of this study as we dive into the book of Revelation. But for now, it's important to remember that God has warned us about this terrible time in both the Old and New Testaments.

REFLECT

1. The Tribulation is one of those biblical concepts that often creates a lot of noise and debate within the church. Who or what have been your primary influences when it comes to understanding the Tribulation and everything it involves?

2. Read Daniel 12:1–13. As you do, underline any verses or phrases that make definitive statements—those that say, "This will happen." What are your overall impressions about those prophetic statements?

3. The angelic beings in Daniel 12 make it clear they are describing events that will occur at "the time of the end" (verse 9). What are some potential benefits of biblical prophecies that point toward our future? How do they help us in the present?

4. When it comes to biblical prophecies that speak of events that have not yet happened, what are some potential challenges or even dangers that we must be aware of when interpreting those passages?

APPLY

5. Many Bible teachers see evidence that the events of the end times, including the Tribulation, are close at hand. How do you respond to that belief?

6. How does the reality of the Tribulation and other end-times events influence your life today? What about for the future?

7. What emotions do you experience when you read through Daniel 12? What about the other passages of Daniel's book that we studied in previous sessions?

8. The prophecies in Daniel 12 point to the future chaos of the Tribulation. They also point to the reality of heaven, which Gabriel described as Daniel's "inheritance at the end of the days" (verse 13). What excites you about the prospect of heaven?

AHEAD

Here's a question I hear often: "How can I believe what the Bible says about the end times?" Many Christians have a pretty good idea what Scripture teaches about the Rapture, the Tribulation, the second coming of Christ, the Millennium, eternity in heaven, and more—they know the major events yet to come on God's eschatological calendar.

Even so, they struggle to trust the somewhat fantastical nature of those events. *People vanishing into thin air? The Antichrist waging war against God Himself? A thousand years of Jesus reigning from Jerusalem over a near-perfect earth? Could such things really happen?*

I understand those doubts to some degree. After all, we live in a world that continually tells us that supernatural things are not possible, let alone real. More, our culture presses us to ridicule even the idea of supernatural events—or else relegate them exclusively to the realm of movies and TV.

But let's get back to the question: "Why should we believe what the Bible says about the end times?" The answer is because biblical prophecies get a perfect score when judged against the record of history. Just look at the book of Daniel. All the events predicted by Daniel came true just as he said they would, even though he lived hundreds of years before them. Biblical prophecy has been proven accurate time and time again. Therefore, we can count on Scripture for the time ahead.

"And there shall be a time of trouble, such as never was since there was a nation, even to that time."

DANIEL 12:1

When this age comes to an end, our world will experience the final week of Gabriel's prophecy—the final seven years—which we often refer to as the "Tribulation."

DAY 10

THE DAY OF THE LORD

Then the Lord *will go forth*
And fight against those nations,
As He fights in the day of battle.
And in that day His feet will stand on the Mount of Olives,
Which faces Jerusalem on the east.
And the Mount of Olives shall be split in two,
From east to west,
Making a very large valley;
Half of the mountain shall move toward the north
And half of it toward the south.

ZECHARIAH 14:3–4

CONTEXT

Zechariah began his life as the son of a priest in Babylon. His family had been among those taken captive from Jerusalem decades earlier, and they had done their best to make a new life in a new city immersed in an entirely different culture. Thankfully, Zechariah was brought up to worship the God of Israel, and he eventually became a priest in his own right. Then, he received a wonderful gift—an opportunity to return to Jerusalem with fifty thousand of his fellow Israelites and resume a proper worship in the promised land.

Unfortunately, Jerusalem had been destroyed. Both its walls and Solomon's magnificent temple were completely undone and thrown down. Rebuilding all that was lost required an enormous financial investment, not to mention a great deal of time and effort. Nehemiah eventually took the lead in rebuilding the city's walls, but it was Zechariah and his fellow prophet Haggai who spearheaded the effort to rebuild the temple. They spent years motivating the people to take on this work, using both chastisements and positive reinforcement.

Throughout his ministry, Zechariah reminded the residents of Jerusalem that their temple would one day be viewed by the Messiah. He urged them to give their best effort in rebuilding God's house. For example: "'Sing and rejoice, O daughter of Zion! For behold, I am coming and I will dwell in your midst,' says the LORD. 'Many nations shall be joined to the LORD in that day, and they shall become My people. And I will dwell in your midst. Then you will know that the LORD of hosts has sent Me to you. And the LORD will take possession of Judah as His inheritance in the Holy Land, and will again choose Jerusalem'" (2:10–12).

Near the end of Zechariah's ministry, he received a prophecy from God that highlighted another day when the Messiah would visit Jerusalem: the Day of the Lord. We often refer to that day as the second coming of Christ. This fateful moment will take place at the end of the Tribulation when Jesus returns, not as the Lamb who takes away the sin of the world, but as the King of kings and Lord of lords.

Throughout the Tribulation, the Antichrist will seek to ensnare the entire world through his satanic government and blasphemous religion. He will seize control of the financial system. He will actively and relentlessly persecute both Christians and Jews, putting millions of people to death because of their newfound faith in Christ. In the end, the Antichrist will gather a huge army near the plains of Megiddo, outside of Jerusalem, in order to destroy the Jewish people once and for all.

At that moment, Christ will return. He will execute judgment against the Antichrist and all who joined his rebellion against God. He will eradicate all evil and establish His millennial kingdom in Jerusalem, where He will reign as the rightful King for a thousand years.

REFLECT

1. As you read through Zechariah 14:1–11, make a note of everything God promised to do or accomplish during this Day of the Lord. Which of those promises feel especially important to you? Why?

2. What makes you feel surprised or confused when you read these verses? What questions come to mind that you would like to have answered?

3. Our modern culture usually pictures Jesus as a gentle and mild-mannered teacher. What are some characteristics of Jesus that are highlighted in Zechariah 14?

4. What Zechariah describes as the Day of the Lord is the same event we often refer to as Armageddon—the final battle of the Tribulation during which the forces of the Antichrist attempt to challenge God Himself. What have you been taught about that final battle?

APPLY

5. One of the primary themes in Zechariah 14 is violence—specifically God's wrath poured out against evildoers. How can we navigate the tension between God as our loving Father and God as the righteous Judge who punishes evil?

6. What are some words you would typically use to describe Jesus, based both on your experience and your reading of Scripture?

7. How do those words compare and contrast to the prophet Zechariah's vision of Jesus as the conquering King in Zechariah 14?

8. When we think about God judging evil and sin, it's easy to forget that our own sins have already been judged and paid for by the sacrifice of Jesus on the cross. What can you do this week to express gratitude and praise for that sacrifice?

AHEAD

"How long, O LORD?" (Psalm 13:1). That's a question asked by many authors of the Old Testament—psalmists, priests, prophets, kings, and more. It's a question we often ask today, as well, especially when it seems as if evil people continue to become more and more successful while those of us trying to do the right thing are regularly pushed aside.

We cry out with the writer of Psalm 94, "LORD, how long will the wicked, how long will the wicked triumph?" (verse 3).

The Day of the Lord is the answer to that question. The promise of a future Day of Judgment is God's guarantee that evil will not triumph in the end. Yes, many people experience consequences for their wickedness today, including through law enforcement and the courts. But we are living in the age of grace. We are living in the period of time God has set aside for the spread of His gospel around the world. For that reason, God's own wrath against evil is often held back.

But not always. And, I think, not for long. Those of us who cry out for justice can take comfort in God's sovereignty and power. Because justice will be done. Evil will be punished. Not only that, evil will ultimately be eradicated. In the same way that Jerusalem will one day be "safely inhabited" (Zechariah 14:11), so will our world finally know true peace.

Behold, the day of the LORD is coming, and your spoil will be divided in your midst.

ZECHARIAH 14:1

The Day of the Lord—the second coming of Christ—will take place at the end of the Tribulation when Jesus returns as the King of kings and Lord of lords.

DAY 11

THE BEGINNING OF SORROWS

"And you will hear of wars and rumors of wars. See that you are not troubled; for all these things must come to pass, but the end is not yet. For nation will rise against nation, and kingdom against kingdom. And there will be famines, pestilences, and earthquakes in various places. All these are the beginning of sorrows."

MATTHEW 24:6–8

CONTEXT

It must have been a lovely sight. After an intense confrontation with the scribes and Pharisees on the temple grounds, Jesus left the city and walked up the Mount of Olives. There He sat down on the side of the hill. Several of His disciples joined him. The view of the city and the temple from that elevated place would have been magnificent.

Perhaps it was that view that inspired the disciples to compliment the physical construction of the temple. Jesus' response was sobering: "Assuredly, I say to you, not one stone shall be left here upon another, that shall not be thrown down" (Matthew 24:2).

The disciples' next question was natural: "Tell us, when will these things be? And what will be the sign of Your coming, and of the end of the age?" (verse 3).

With that as a launching point, Jesus began what scholars today refer to as the Olivet Discourse. For two chapters, the Son of Man opened a doorway to the future and described—sometimes in surprising detail—what will happen leading up to the end of the age. He also described what will happen during the Tribulation and at the final judgment of humanity.

One of the critical elements of Jesus' teaching during this time is what scholars often call the "birth pains principle." It comes from this passage: "You will hear of wars and rumors of wars, but see to it that you are not alarmed. Such things must happen, but the end is still to come. Nation will rise against nation, and kingdom against kingdom. There will be famines and earthquakes in various places. All these are the beginning of birth pains" (verses 6–8 NIV).

That phrase "birth pains" at the end of verse 8 is a key. The Greek term there is *odin*, which does indeed describe the contractions that occur during the process of giving birth. So you might be wondering, *What do birth pains have to do with prophecies about the end of the world?* The answer is quite stunning.

In describing the events that will take place leading up to the end of the age, Jesus mentioned wars, rumors of war, famines, earthquakes, and pestilences. Obviously, each item on that list has been part of human history for as long as there has been human history. We've always had them, and we will continue to experience them right up until the moment when God chooses to turn the page on His eschatological calendar.

Jesus' point, however, is that wars, earthquakes, famines, and plagues will increase dramatically as we approach the final days. During childbirth, contractions become both more frequent and more intense as the time of delivery draws near. In the same way, the "signs" of the end will become more frequent and more intense as we move closer to the end of this age.

Let's look more closely at how Jesus' prophecy from the Olivet Discourse sets the context for our understanding of the end times.

REFLECT

1. Take a few minutes to read Matthew 24:3–14 out loud. What strikes you as most interesting or most important from that passage? Why?

2. How would you explain the "birth pains principle" in your own words? What does it mean, and how does it apply to our lives as we try to prepare for what may happen in the future?

3. Jesus mentioned "false prophets" as a sign of the last days. What makes false teachers within the church as dangerous as earthquakes, wars, and pestilence (plagues)?

4. Jesus offered a parable in verses 32–35 to help the disciples understand what He was saying—the parable of the fig tree. How would you summarize the point of that parable? How does it connect with the "birth pains principle"?

APPLY

5. So far in this study, we've primarily explored passages of Scripture containing prophecies that have already come true—the restoration of Israel as a nation, for example. How comfortable do you feel exploring biblical prophecies about events that are still unfulfilled? Why?

6. What are some of the big questions you wrestle with when it comes to the future and the eventual "end of the world"?

7. What are some ways you have attempted to find answers to those questions?

8. Jesus mentioned false prophets, wars, famines, pestilences, and earthquakes as "signs" that the end of this age is drawing near. To what degree has your life been impacted by those types of events?

AHEAD

Let's go back to Jesus sitting on Mount Olivet with His disciples. Remember that in responding to their admiration of the temple, He told them, "Assuredly, I say to you, not one stone shall be left here upon another, that shall not be thrown down" (Matthew 24:2). This is where the principle of layers within biblical prophecy comes into play again.

In AD 70, about forty years after Jesus sat on that hillside with His disciples, the Roman general Titus laid siege to Jerusalem. He was under orders from the emperor to end the rebellion in that region, and he took drastic steps to do so. His soldiers fell on the city with terrible ferocity, slaughtering men, women, and children alike. Those same soldiers also destroyed the temple as a testament to the power of Rome. Using innovative techniques, they first burned the temple and then used pry bars to split apart every massive stone within its walls.

Just as Jesus predicted forty years earlier, not one stone of the temple was left upon another. The entire edifice was cast down.

In warning His disciples about the short-term threat to both Jerusalem and the temple, Jesus also warned humanity about the much greater (and much longer-term) destruction that would take place during the Tribulation. His accuracy about the former gives us confidence that what He told us about the end times will also come to pass.

"Then they will deliver you up to tribulation and kill you, and you will be hated by all nations for My name's sake."

MATTHEW 24:9

Jesus, in warning His disciples about the threat to Jerusalem and the temple, also warned humanity about the much greater destruction that would take place during the Tribulation.

DAY 12

SHEEP AND GOATS

"When the Son of Man comes in His glory, and all the holy angels with Him, then He will sit on the throne of His glory. All the nations will be gathered before Him, and He will separate them one from another, as a shepherd divides his sheep from the goats. And He will set the sheep on His right hand, but the goats on the left."

MATTHEW 25:31–33

CONTEXT

What are some words you would use to describe Jesus? When I ask that question in a church or small-group setting, I usually hear a lot of descriptors about His titles: "Savior," "Son of Man," "Messiah," and so on. I also hear a lot of adjectives that focus on His goodness: "loving," "gentle," "kind," "compassionate," and more.

All of these are true. Every word listed above is thoroughly supported by what we learn about Jesus in the Gospels and elsewhere. He is certainly loving and good and compassionate and merciful, plus many other similar adjectives. These all fit with His role as the Lamb of God who takes away the sin of the world.

There is another side to Jesus, however, that we often overlook. In the same way that He is our Savior and Healer, Christ is also our King. In fact, He is the King of kings and Lord of lords. More than that, He is our Judge. As such, He values not only mercy and grace but also justice. And yes, even wrath.

These are the aspects of the Messiah's character that Jesus Himself emphasized when describing His role and His mindset at the end of the age.

As we saw in Day 11, Matthew 24–25 records Jesus' final sermon during His public ministry, which is often called the Olivet Discourse. This wasn't a regular sermon, however. It was laser-focused on the end times. In those two chapters, Jesus described the "signs" that will herald the end of our current age and usher in the Rapture, followed immediately by the Tribulation.

In Matthew 24:15–28, Jesus offered several striking details about the seven years of the Tribulation, although He focused primarily on the final three and a half years of that time period, which are often called the "Great Tribulation." The Antichrist will squeeze the whole world in those days in an effort to completely destroy all Christians and every last vestige of the Jewish people.

Yet he will not succeed. Why? Because Jesus Christ will return to our world at the end of the Tribulation. He will return not as a merciful Savior but as our righteous King. He will reenter our atmosphere with wrath and judgment and fury.

As we move to Matthew 25, Jesus relayed two parables to His disciples there on the side of Mount Olivet: the parable of the wise and foolish virgins, along with the parable of the talents—one of His most famous stories. Then, in verses 31–46, He described the process He will use to separate the righteous from the unrighteous during that great and terrible day.

REFLECT

1. Start this exploration of Matthew 25 by reading the parable of the wise and foolish virgins in verses 1–13. How would you summarize the main point of that parable? What was Jesus teaching His disciples (and us)?

2. Look also at the parable of the talents in verses 14–30. What is the typical lesson we take from this parable when we talk about it in church or small groups? How does it change your understanding of the parable to see it placed in the middle of Jesus' teaching about the end times?

3. As mentioned above, verses 31–46 describe what will happen when Jesus returns in triumph at the end of the Tribulation period. What can we learn about Jesus' nature and character from these verses?

4. Jesus' words in verse 41 can be especially jarring: "Depart from Me, you cursed, into the everlasting fire prepared for the devil and his angels." How should we understand the biblical concept of hell? How can we teach about that reality in a way that is loving and helpful?

APPLY

5. It's not pleasant to read about Jesus separating "sheep" from "goats"—meaning, those who are saved from those who are not. What emotions do you experience when you read about that separation of the righteous from the unrighteous?

6. As it currently stands, would you be considered a "sheep" (a member of God's kingdom) or a "goat"? Explain your answer.

7. The parables in Matthew 25 encourage all people to "watch" and prepare themselves for the events that will take place at the end of this age. What does it look like for you to be watchful in that way?

8. What is one change you can make this week that would show that you really believe that Jesus is King of kings and Lord of lords?

AHEAD

At the end of the Tribulation, Jesus will personally separate those who received His free gift of salvation from those who did not. That brings up an important point about salvation itself. In Matthew 25, Jesus praises those who are members of His kingdom for their good works: In His words, "For I was hungry and you gave Me food; I was thirsty and you gave Me drink; I was a stranger and you took Me in; I was naked and you clothed Me; I was sick and you visited Me; I was in prison and you came to Me" (verses 35–36).

Jesus' emphasis on the kindness and compassion of His followers sometimes leads people to wonder, *Is that what makes a person saved? Bringing food to the hungry and visiting prisoners and that kind of thing?*

The answer is no, and we know that from the broader message of Scripture. For example: "For by grace you have been saved through faith, and that not of yourselves; it is the gift of God, not of works, lest anyone should boast" (Ephesians 2:8–9).

Salvation is a free gift from God that we receive through faith, not by doing "good works." Still, those who are saved will demonstrate their righteousness by living like Jesus, which does include loving and serving and caring for others. That is what Jesus highlighted in Matthew 25.

"All the nations will be gathered before Him,
and He will separate them one from another, as a shepherd
divides his sheep from the goats."

MATTHEW 25:32

At the end of the Tribulation, Jesus will separate those who
received His free gift of salvation from those who did not.

DAY 13

THE PROMISE OF HEAVEN

"In My Father's house are many mansions; if it were not so, I would have told you. I go to prepare a place for you. And if I go and prepare a place for you, I will come again and receive you to Myself; that where I am, there you may be also."

JOHN 14:2–3

CONTEXT

It was the last night of Jesus' earthly ministry. The same night He was betrayed, arrested, and tried by the hostile Sanhedrin. Before those events, however, Jesus gathered with His disciples in the upper room to share a meal together. The Passover Feast was a celebration of the way God protected and preserved His people during the exodus from Egypt. It's appropriate, then, that Jesus used that feast to teach His disciples about God's protection and preservation of His people for eternity.

Jesus began His teaching in John 14 by saying, "Let not your heart be troubled; you believe in God, believe also in Me" (verse 1). The disciples had good reasons to be troubled. Mainly, Jesus had told them on several occasions that He was going away—even that He would be killed. Most of the disciples still expected the Messiah to lead a military revolt against Rome; therefore, Jesus' words were deeply confusing. And yes, troubling.

Jesus' response was an encouragement to "believe." Specifically, to believe He is who they knew Him to be. The Messiah. The Christ. God in human flesh.

On the basis of that belief, Jesus offered what is perhaps the most important prophetic promise in all of Scripture: "In My Father's house are many mansions; if it were not so, I would have told you. I go to prepare a place for you. And if I go and prepare a place for you, I will come again and receive you to Myself; that where I am, there you may be also" (verses 2–3).

I want to focus on two key words in that prophecy, and the first is *mansions*. In the original Greek language, the word translated "mansion" simply means a place to stay, a dwelling, or a home. It doesn't specifically refer to a large, ornate, palatial estate—the kind of image we associate with "mansions" today. That's why other translations say, "In My Father's house are many rooms."

What's important is that these mansions or dwelling places or rooms are connected to the Father. They are specifically connected to the "house" where God's presence dwells, which means they are in heaven. And that makes them more glorious than any mansion we might ever encounter here on earth!

The second word that's worth highlighting is *place*. Jesus said that He was going to prepare a "place" for His disciples, including Christians today. That word in the original Greek is *topos*, which always refers to a specific, literal, physical location. Heaven is not a state of mind. Heaven is not a realm of elevated consciousness. Heaven is not a journey with no final destination.

Heaven is a place. And Jesus' prophetic promise is that He will one day return to take us home.

REFLECT

1. Read John 14:1–6 out loud. What specific promises did Jesus make in those verses?

2. As mentioned earlier, Jesus spoke those words on the final night of His earthly ministry—the night before His crucifixion. How does that reality influence your understanding of what Jesus said—including what He promised?

3. Human history began in a specific place (*topos*) that provided a physical connection with God the Father. Read Genesis 2:8–25 to learn more about life in the garden of Eden. How does that passage shape or influence what you expect to experience in heaven?

4. Next, take a look at Revelation 21:1–8, which describes the establishment of a "new heaven" and "new earth." What can we learn from that passage about what heaven will be like?

APPLY

5. It's easy to think of heaven as an abstract concept—something that is separate from our "real" lives here on earth. What are some ways heaven can motivate your actions and attitudes today?

6. What are the primary ideas or images that come to mind when you think about heaven? What do you expect to experience there?

7. How has your understanding of heaven shifted over time? How does your picture of heaven today compare with your picture of heaven from earlier in your life?

8. Verse 6 can be difficult for many in our culture to hear: "I am the way, the truth, and the life. No one comes to the Father except through Me." Where do you have an opportunity to take a stand on that truth this week?

AHEAD

When reading through John 14:1–6, there's one passage that often makes people feel uncomfortable in today's culture. After Thomas tells Jesus that he and the other disciples don't know the way to where He is going, Jesus reminds them that He is the way to heaven—and He alone. In His words, "No one comes to the Father except through Me" (verse 6).

You may wonder, *Isn't it arrogant for Christians to say that Jesus is the only way? Isn't it arrogant to say that we are correct and all other religions are incorrect?*

I understand the emotions behind those questions. We all want to be fair, and we don't want to be seen as haughty or conceited in a culture that values tolerance above almost anything else. Thankfully, the answer to those questions is a hearty "no." It is not arrogant for a servant to believe the words of his Master. It is not arrogant for a disciple to repeat the words of her Teacher. In the same way, we are not arrogant when we believe and repeat the truths that God has revealed through Scripture.

Therefore, let us never be ashamed to affirm the words of Jesus: "I am the way, the truth, and the life. No one comes to the Father except through Me."

"And if I go and prepare a place for you, I will come again and receive you to Myself; that where I am, there you may be also."

JOHN 14:3

Heaven is a place—and Jesus' prophetic promise is that He will one day return to take us home.

DAY 14

HATRED AND PERSECUTION

"These things I have spoken to you, that you should not be made to stumble. They will put you out of the synagogues; yes, the time is coming that whoever kills you will think that he offers God service. And these things they will do to you because they have not known the Father nor Me. But these things I have told you, that when the time comes, you may remember that I told you of them."

JOHN 16:1–4

CONTEXT

We don't have a lot of information about the lives of Jesus' disciples before they became disciples, although we do know some information. James and John were fishermen, for example. So were Simon and Andrew. We know Matthew (formerly Levi) was a tax collector, which means he was despised by most in the Jewish community as a collaborator with Rome. We also know another disciple named Simon was a Zealot, which means he functioned almost as a terrorist in opposition to the Roman occupation of Israel.

It's safe to say the disciples were a diverse group of individuals. One thing they did have in common, though, was their lack of qualification to be disciples. You see, in that day, all young Jewish boys went to school to learn about Torah and the history of their people. But most of those boys stopped attending school at the age of thirteen. That's when they became apprentices, usually with their fathers as part of the family trade.

Only the brightest of students continued to study past the age of thirteen—the best of the best. Those who continued to do well were apprenticed to a local rabbi. They learned his interpretations of Torah, served him, and traveled with him from town to town when he taught.

Importantly, none of Jesus' disciples were in this group. None of His disciples were among the best of the best at school. That's why they took up fishing and other trades. And that's why it was such a surprise when Jesus called them to follow Him as He began His public ministry.

It must have been quite a change for the disciples when Jesus began to grow in popularity. Most of the disciples were regular guys—just normal members of the community. But all of a sudden they were traveling with this Rabbi who performed miracle after miracle. He healed the sick, including lepers. He gave sight to the blind. He caused those who were lame to walk. He cast out demons. He even raised the dead! The disciples were part of those events.

Imagine what it must have been like for the disciples on the day of the triumphal entry. They traveled with Jesus to Jerusalem and encountered huge crowds of people cheering for Jesus and singing praises to Him. "Hosanna to God in the highest!" The disciples were caught up in that praise. All of a sudden, they were like local celebrities. People knew they were connected to Jesus, which means they had status. And approval. And even envy.

With all that in mind, think of what it must have been like for the disciples when Jesus said these words during the Last Supper: "They will put you out of the synagogues; yes, the time is coming that whoever kills you will think that he offers God service" (John 16:2).

Let's take a closer look at the whiplash of Jesus' prophetic claims—and how that prophecy applies to Christians today.

REFLECT

1. Look more closely at John 15:18–16:4. How would you describe the main message Jesus wanted to communicate in those verses?

2. Which elements of Jesus' warning to His disciples were prophetic? Meaning, which parts of those verses pointed forward to future events?

3. Verses 18–25 in chapter 15 describe the hatred expressed by "the world" toward Jesus, both during His ministry and after. What are some possible explanations for that hatred? In other words, why does so much of our culture despise Jesus and what He teaches?

4. Read Acts 5:17–32 to see a small example of how Jesus' prophecy was fulfilled. Where do you see similar persecution or harassment of Christians in today's world?

APPLY

5. Jesus' prophetic words were fulfilled in the lives of His disciples given that most of them died by violence. How should Christians respond today when they are persecuted or even threatened with death because of their faith in Christ?

6. To what degree has your life been affected by the "hatred" of the world, or even active persecution from those who oppose Jesus and His kingdom?

7. When was the most recent time you were made to feel uncomfortable or attacked because of your faith? What emotions did you experience in that moment? How did you respond?

8. How would you like to respond if and when you are targeted as "hateful" because of your faith in Jesus? What would you like to say, and what would you like to do if that moment comes?

AHEAD

When we think about concepts such as persecution or martyrdom, it's natural to connect them with the past. We know the stories of many Jesus followers who were killed because of their faith—from Stephen to the apostle Paul to Polycarp to Jan Hus to William Tyndale to Nate Saint and more. Their stories are both compelling and inspirational.

Unfortunately, Christian martyrdom is not an issue relegated to the past. Instead, it's very much a part of our present. In fact, scholars have identified the twentieth century as the bloodiest in history in terms of Christians being killed for their faith—and the twenty-first century is already shaping up to be even worse.

All around the world today, people live in fear because of their faith in Christ. People are harassed, disenfranchised, robbed, and even killed because they claim Jesus as their Savior. It happens in China and North Korea. It happens in African nations such as Somalia and Nigeria. It happens in Middle Eastern nations including Iran and Afghanistan. But it also happens in Europe. And India. And the United States.

Jesus told us we will experience trouble in this world—that we will be hated and harassed and even killed. Because that prophecy is yet being fulfilled, we must support one another as members of His church.

"Remember the word that I said to you, 'A servant is not greater than his master.' If they persecuted Me, they will also persecute you."

JOHN 15:20

Jesus told us that we will experience trouble in this world—and because that prophecy is yet being fulfilled, we must support one another as members of His church.

DAY 15

RAISED IN GLORY

So also is the resurrection of the dead. The body is sown in corruption, it is raised in incorruption. It is sown in dishonor, it is raised in glory. It is sown in weakness, it is raised in power. It is sown a natural body, it is raised a spiritual body. There is a natural body, and there is a spiritual body.

1 CORINTHIANS 15:42–44

CONTEXT

The city of Corinth was famous in the ancient world. Or, perhaps more accurately, the city was infamous. Located smack in the middle of a major trade route in southern Greece, Corinth was an exceedingly prosperous city. It had great wealth and prestige. Unfortunately, it also had a reputation for debauchery that bordered on the extreme.

When the apostle Paul first traveled to the city of Corinth as part of his second missionary journey, he spent almost two years planting a church there and working faithfully to train up its members in the way they should go. He worked diligently to help the Corinthian Christians separate themselves from the vileness of their culture and instead cling to the values of God's kingdom. He succeeded in many ways, yet there were a number of obstacles that continued to plague the church—especially after Paul left to continue his missionary journeys.

For those reasons, it's no surprise that Paul's epistles to the Christians in Corinth were mainly focused on correcting errors and offering guidance to help those believers get back on track. Apparently, one of the areas in which the Corinthians needed specific guidance was the concept of resurrection from the dead.

Paul wrote, "Now if Christ is preached that He has been raised from the dead, how do some among you say that there is no resurrection of the dead? But if there is no resurrection of the dead, then Christ is not risen. And if Christ is not risen, then our preaching is empty and your faith is also empty" (1 Corinthians 15:12–14).

Some in the Corinthian church resisted the concept of people being raised from the dead. Likely, this was the result of a pagan belief called *dualism* that was common at the time. According to dualism, the physical parts of our world (and our bodies) are generally unclean; they are base and profane. In contrast, the spiritual realm (including our spiritual selves) is connected to the divine; whatever is spiritual is noble and good.

Given that belief, it's easy to see why some of the Corinthian believers recoiled at the idea of being physically resurrected from the dead—even in the case of Jesus. The concept of a dead person being "raised again" would have been reprehensible to those who were grounded in dualism. They pictured it in the same way we might picture zombies.

In order to correct this theological misunderstanding, Paul wrote 1 Corinthians 15—which many theologians describe as the "Resurrection Chapter" of the Bible. As we look closely at verses 35–49, we'll see Paul making several prophetic promises about what all Christians will experience through our own resurrection in the future.

REFLECT

1. As you read 1 Corinthians 15:35–49, pay attention to the different ways Paul explained the concept of people being raised from the dead. How would you summarize the overall point Paul was making in that passage?

2. Perhaps because of the influence of dualism, Paul went to great pains to explain how our resurrected bodies will be different from our physical bodies. What are some of those differences?

3. Verses 46–49 offer a comparison between Adam (the first man) and Jesus (the heavenly Man). What does that comparison teach us about our future resurrection after the moment of physical death?

4. Jesus also addressed the question of resurrection when He was confronted by the Sadducees, who claimed there is no afterlife. Read Matthew 22:23–33 to see that confrontation. What was Jesus' argument in support of resurrection?

APPLY

5. By proclaiming the truth that Christians will be raised to new life even after their physical bodies pass away, Paul was speaking prophetically about the future of every believer alive today. To what degree does your future resurrection and glorification influence your present life? Your present choices?

6. The culture of Paul's day embraced the idea that physical bodies are unclean or profane. How would you summarize our culture's view of the human body today? What about your own view?

7. Your body is a gift from God in the present. On a practical level, what does it look like for you to be a good steward of that gift?

8. You will one day have a celestial, heavenly body built for eternity. Given that promise, what are some dangers of focusing too much on your current, earthly body?

AHEAD

One of the bigger misconceptions people hold about the afterlife is that heaven will be filled with disembodied spirits floating around in the clouds. We know people are made up of more than flesh and bones—we have a spirit and a soul. But there is a misconception that *only* our spirits and souls will be present in heaven. That we will no longer possess a physical body once we die and are translated to heaven.

Ironically, that belief is a repurposing of the dualistic thinking Paul was trying to correct within the Corinthian church. The idea that heaven is not for physical bodies has persisted for thousands of years.

According to Paul, when a Christian's physical body dies, "it is sown a natural body, it is raised a spiritual body. There is a natural body, and there is a spiritual body" (verse 44). There is not a natural body and a spirit, but instead a "spiritual body."

What is a spiritual body? Put simply, while our natural bodies are designed and suited for life on earth, a spiritual body is designed and suited for eternity with God in heaven. Such bodies will be glorious, incorruptible, powerful, and eternal. That is what awaits us after death!

As was the man of dust, so also are those who are made of dust; and as is the heavenly Man, so also are those who are heavenly.

1 CORINTHIANS 15:48

Our spiritual bodies—glorious, incorruptible, powerful—are designed and suited for eternity with God in heaven.

DAY 16

THE RAPTURE

For the Lord Himself will descend from heaven with a shout, with the voice of an archangel, and with the trumpet of God. And the dead in Christ will rise first. Then we who are alive and remain shall be caught up together with them in the clouds to meet the Lord in the air. And thus we shall always be with the Lord.

1 THESSALONIANS 4:16–17

CONTEXT

According to Acts 17, Paul founded the church in Thessalonica during a brief stay in that city. Why was it brief? Paul preached in the synagogue for three Sabbaths in a row, as was his custom. He typically approached the Jewish population first when visiting a new city. After that third message, however, some of the Jews became enraged and started a mob that set the city in an uproar. Paul was forced to flee in the middle of the night. Still, he kept in contact with the church leaders in Thessalonica through regular correspondence, including the epistles we know as 1 and 2 Thessalonians.

During his time in Thessalonica, Paul emphasized the prophetic event we know as the Rapture—that at some moment in the future Jesus will step out of God's throne room in heaven and gather to Himself all who have received the free gift of salvation. This is a key part of the gospel message, as we saw in Day 13. When Jesus ascended to heaven, He promised to one day return and bring His disciples to His Father's house (John 14:1–6).

The Thessalonian believers were enraptured (pun intended) by Paul's message. They were gripped by the reality of the Rapture, and they deeply desired to witness that event in their lifetimes. In fact, they were so adamant about this desire that they began to mourn and grieve for fellow believers who had already passed away, thinking that those believers had missed the Rapture—that they would be left out of it somehow.

Some of the Thessalonians were even worried that missing the Rapture was the same as missing heaven itself. They were under the impression that only those who were alive on the day of the Rapture would be welcomed by Jesus into heaven. Thankfully, Paul took the time to correct this misunderstanding in 1 Thessalonians 4:13–18. In that passage, he emphasized four key truths about salvation in general and the Rapture specifically:

- At the Rapture, God will gather everyone who has received the gospel through faith, including those believers who have already passed away. (In the words of the passage, those who "sleep" in death.)
- On the actual day of the Rapture, those who already died will rise first. They will receive new heavenly bodies.
- Believers who are alive on the day of the Rapture will be "caught up" with Jesus in the clouds. In some way, they will vanish from our world and be transported to heaven.
- Every person who has accepted the gift of salvation will remain with God for eternity.

Keep these truths in mind as we take a deeper look at the doctrine of the Rapture.

REFLECT

1. The Rapture can be somewhat confusing because different denominations point to different moments in the future when it will occur. How would you describe the doctrine of the Rapture to someone who has never heard about it?

2. Look again at 1 Thessalonians 4:13–18. What is it about the doctrine of the Rapture that would "comfort" those who were grieving?

3. Take another look at John 14:1–6. What are some ways Jesus' teaching in those verses was pointing to the Rapture?

4. Previously we looked at 1 Corinthians 15:35–49. Now, take a look at verses 51–58. How do those verses add to your understanding of what the Rapture is and how it will unfold?

APPLY

5. Both Paul and the Christians in Thessalonica believed the Rapture could happen at any moment; they expected it to happen during their lifetimes. How would that kind of expectation and anticipation have influenced their daily lives?

6. What are some benefits of focusing on the Rapture and anticipating that future moment? Are there any risks to devoting a lot of energy to that anticipation?

7. The Thessalonians experienced "sorrow" because of the death of their fellow believers. When was the last time you experienced the loss of someone you love? How did you feel in that moment? How do you feel about that loss now?

8. How would you advise others to navigate the tension between grieving Christians who pass away and celebrating your future reunion at the Rapture?

AHEAD

I've mentioned God's "eschatological calendar" a few times in these pages. By that I mean the series of events that God has declared will take place throughout the end times. Those events include the Rapture, the Tribulation, the second coming of Jesus, the Millennium, the re-forging of the universe into a new heaven and a new earth, and the eternal state we often refer to as eternity in heaven.

The Rapture is the next event on that calendar. When it happens, the Rapture will mark the final page of the current age in biblical history—what we sometimes call the church age or the age of grace—and the first page of the seven-year Tribulation. It will also be a major event in terms of the world stage, as tens or hundreds of millions of Christians are "caught up" to heaven by Christ.

Importantly, the Rapture is an imminent event. That doesn't mean it will happen soon—not necessarily. But it does mean there are no other events that need to take place before the Rapture. Therefore, what the Thessalonians desired to see could occur at any moment.

Let's all take heed of that truth!

For if we believe that Jesus died and rose again, even so God will bring with Him those who sleep in Jesus.

1 THESSALONIANS 4:14

The message of the gospel is that every person *who has accepted the gift of salvation will remain with God for eternity.*

DAY 17

A THIEF IN THE NIGHT

For you yourselves know perfectly that the day of the Lord so comes as a thief in the night. For when they say, 'Peace and safety!' then sudden destruction comes upon them, as labor pains upon a pregnant woman. And they shall not escape.

1 THESSALONIANS 5:2–3

CONTEXT

When studying Scripture, transitional words and phrases are important: "therefore," "but," "and so," and the like. We find an especially important transitional word at the beginning of 1 Thessalonians 5. As we saw in Day 16, Paul made it a point to address a few misconceptions the Christians in Thessalonica believed about the Rapture. Namely, they were afraid that those who died physically before the Rapture would not be gathered by Jesus and taken to heaven. Therefore, they grieved terribly whenever one of their number passed away. Paul corrected their thinking by teaching them that, at the moment of the Rapture, Jesus would gather all who believed in Him—including both the living and the dead.

That was at the end of 1 Thessalonians 4. Then comes the transition at the beginning of chapter 5: "*But* concerning the times and the seasons, brethren, you have no need that I should write to you" (verse 1, emphasis added). The word "but" shows that Paul was changing topics within his letter. (Remember, the original epistles weren't divided into chapters.) At the end of chapter 4, Paul finished talking about the Rapture as a positive event for those who know Jesus and would be "caught up" into His presence. Here at the beginning of chapter 5, Paul began talking about the Day of the Lord as a negative event for those who reject God and will therefore experience His judgment.

As we saw on Day 10, the Day of the Lord refers generally to a time in the future when God will decisively punish those who choose to rebel against Him and embrace evil. More specifically, this "day" refers to the moment when Jesus returns at the end of the Tribulation. On that day, the King of kings and Lord of lords will return to our world and crush the evil kingdom of the Antichrist. He will pronounce judgment on those who follow Satan, and He will destroy them in His wrath.

When speaking about this day of judgment, Paul twice described its arrival as "a thief," or "a thief in the night." That's a powerful image, and it speaks to the ignorance of the world when it comes to God's expectations—and the consequences for ignoring those expectations.

Prior to the Rapture, most people will be going about their lives focused only on their goals, their desires, and their priorities. They will have little to no thought for God, and they will be shocked by the spectacle of the Rapture. Those same people will again pursue their own selfish goals during the Tribulation. Many will work to oppose God and His kingdom. Therefore, they will be caught off guard when Christ returns as King. They won't see it coming, just as people who sleep deeply at night don't see a thief when he breaks into the house.

Let's talk about what this principle means, not only for the world, but also for those of us who are currently members of God's kingdom.

REFLECT

1. Read through 1 Thessalonians 5:1–11 to see the full scope of Paul's teaching about this subject. How would you summarize the primary message he was communicating to the Christians in Thessalonica through those verses?

2. As we've seen, the Day of the Lord always refers to a moment when God's wrath is poured out against evil and unrighteousness. Where do you see evil and unrighteousness in the world today that seem to be unpunished? How do you respond to that seeming lack of consequences?

3. Look specifically at verse 3. Where do you see people in our culture crying out "peace and safety!"? Meaning, where do you see people or organizations believing themselves to be safe from God's judgment and wrath?

4. While nonbelievers go about their lives in ignorance of God's judgment, Paul called believers to "watch and be sober" (verse 6). What does that look like on a practical level?

APPLY

5. The Bible makes it clear that God will punish evil in His own timing. Do you think Christians today have a role in carrying out God's wrath or judging those who have rejected Him? Why or why not?

6. What does it look like for you to "watch and be sober" in the various spheres of your life? At home, for example? At work? Online?

7. Paul commanded us to put on "the breastplate of faith and love" (verse 8). When have you recently had an opportunity to demonstrate faith in God? What happened next in that situation?

8. The world will be calling out "peace and safety!" when the time of God's judgment arrives. They will be complacent. Where do you have an opportunity to raise the alarm in your community about the reality of God's judgment? In your home?

AHEAD

One of the big questions scholars wrestle with in theological circles is whether Christians will be present during the Tribulation. Apparently the Thessalonian believers wondered about that as well. Would they endure the pain and chaos of God's judgment against the world?

Thankfully, Paul offered a direct answer to their questions: "For God did not appoint us to wrath, but to obtain salvation through our Lord Jesus Christ, who died for us, that whether we wake or sleep, we should live together with Him" (verses 9–10).

If you have accepted the free gift of salvation through faith in Jesus Christ, then you are not appointed to wrath. Meaning, you will not experience the terrors of the Day of the Lord here on earth. That's because you will either pass away prior to that season of wrath, or you will be raptured immediately before it begins. Either way, those who are Christians on this side of the Rapture will not endure the Tribulation.

Still, it's helpful to follow Paul's advice to "watch and be sober" in terms of our own struggle against sin. When we're not careful, unrighteousness can still slip into our hearts like a thief in the night and cause damage in our lives. Therefore, we should live each day in the light of God's Word and the direction of His Spirit.

But you, brethren, are not in darkness, so that this Day should overtake you as a thief.

1 THESSALONIANS 5:4

As believers in Christ, we must live each day in the light of God's Word and the direction of His Spirit.

DAY 18

EVERLASTING DESTRUCTION

These shall be punished with everlasting destruction from the presence of the Lord and from the glory of His power, when He comes, in that Day, to be glorified in His saints and to be admired among all those who believe, because our testimony among you was believed.

2 THESSALONIANS 1:9–10

CONTEXT

As a reminder, Paul was able to stay in Thessalonica for only a little more than three weeks during his second missionary journey. That's because his teaching in the synagogue made one group of Jews so angry that they started a riot, which ultimately led to Paul fleeing the city for his life. As we move into 2 Thessalonians, it becomes clear that Paul wasn't the only one who endured persecution. Apparently the believers who remained in that city also began to be harassed because of their faith.

Paul began his second epistle by praising the Thessalonian Christians for their faith and their love demonstrated toward each other—especially given the level of pain they were experiencing. Paul commended their patience "in all your persecutions and tribulations that you endure" (verse 4). He acknowledged their willingness to "suffer" for the kingdom of God (verse 5), and that many in the community caused "trouble" for the church (verse 6).

It's important to highlight the Thessalonian Christians weren't complaining about this suffering. They didn't write to Paul and ask why a good God would allow them to experience persecution, nor did they express a desire for vengeance on those who troubled them. Instead, Paul noted that the Thessalonian church endured their suffering with "patience" (verse 4).

Even so, Paul assured his readers that there would come a day when the evil actions of their oppressors would be punished. God Himself would "repay with tribulation those who trouble you" (verse 6). As we saw previously, this is the Day of the Lord, when Christ returns as King to conquer the forces of evil and establish His kingdom over all the earth. In that day, all believers (including the Thessalonians) will be vindicated and established in the bliss of Christ's millennial kingdom, which we will explore in more detail later in these pages.

But what about those who don't believe? What will be the eternal fate of those who reject the gospel and God's free gift of salvation—both now and during the Tribulation? According to Paul, "These shall be punished with everlasting destruction from the presence of the Lord and from the glory of His power" (verse 9).

This, of course, is the doctrine of hell. Those who refuse salvation will be denied the wonders of the Millennium and of eternal life in heaven. Instead, they will be separated from God for eternity—not because God is cruel or unjust but because they chose not to accept God's love and kindness.

Yet please remember that hell is more than a doctrine. These verses are prophetic. Meaning, they are declarations of what will happen in the future. All who say no to Jesus will experience not only judgment on the future Day of the Lord but also eternal punishment in hell. God's Word has declared it to be so; therefore, it will be so.

REFLECT

1. As you read through 2 Thessalonians 1:1–12, underline specific words or phrases that are connected with the concept of hell. How would you describe hell to someone who has never heard of that concept before?

2. Our culture has a lot to say about the topic of the afterlife, including the possibility of hell. What are some of the main messages communicated about hell in our entertainment media? What about our academic thinkers? What about politicians and other thought leaders?

3. Jesus spoke about hell through His parable of the wheat and the tares. Read that parable in Matthew 13:24–30. Also read Jesus' explanation in verses 36–43. How do those passages add to your understanding of what hell is and what it means?

4. Jesus also addressed the reality of hell at the end of His Olivet Discourse. Read Matthew 25:31–46. How does that passage add to your understanding of hell?

APPLY

5. It's a truth often emphasized in Scripture that hell is as real as heaven. In fact, both are versions of eternity. How does that reality impact your faith in God? How does it impact your everyday life?

6. What do you believe about hell? Be specific in describing your thoughts on whether it exists, who goes there, what happens there, and so on.

7. How has your understanding of the doctrine of hell changed over the course of your lifetime? What have been the main shifts (if any) in your beliefs about hell?

8. Followers of Jesus need have no personal fear of hell. Instead, the reality of hell should motivate us to spread the gospel. Think of someone who needs to hear the message of salvation. How will you pray for that person this week?

AHEAD

As mentioned earlier, the believers in Thessalonica were forced to deal with a culture that was hostile both to the gospel message and to them as individuals. Yet they chose to endure that hostility with patience and with faith.

In commending the Thessalonians, Paul wrote, "Therefore we also pray always for you that our God would count you worthy of this calling, and fulfill all the good pleasure of His goodness and the work of faith with power, *that the name of our Lord Jesus Christ may be glorified in you, and you in Him*, according to the grace of our God and the Lord Jesus Christ" (2 Thessalonians 1:11–12, emphasis added).

We also live in a culture that is largely hostile to faith in God. Our culture is hostile to the Bible, including the claim that Jesus alone is the way to salvation. Our culture is hostile even to the concept of a God who created us—and who therefore has authority over our lives.

Because of that hostility, you and I have an opportunity to glorify Christ just as the Thessalonians did. May we take advantage of that opportunity each day!

It is a righteous thing with God to repay with tribulation those who trouble you, and to give you who are troubled rest with us when the Lord Jesus is revealed from heaven.

2 THESSALONIANS 1:6–7

Jesus will return to conquer the forces of evil and establish His kingdom on earth. On that day, all believers will be vindicated and established in His millennial kingdom.

DAY 19

PERILOUS TIMES WILL COME

But know this, that in the last days perilous times will come: For men will be lovers of themselves, lovers of money, boasters, proud, blasphemers, disobedient to parents, unthankful, unholy, unloving, unforgiving, slanderers, without self-control, brutal, despisers of good, traitors, headstrong, haughty, lovers of pleasure rather than lovers of God, having a form of godliness but denying its power. And from such people turn away!

2 TIMOTHY 3:1–5

CONTEXT

The New Testament contains two letters written from the apostle Paul to a young man named Timothy, who was one of Paul's key protégés. On the outside, the circumstances during which Paul wrote those letters seem similar—mainly because the apostle was imprisoned in Rome on both occasions. Yet a deeper look shows that Paul wrote 1 Timothy when he was basically confined to house arrest. He was able to receive visitors and was active in the life of the Roman church.

The circumstances surrounding the epistle we know as 2 Timothy are much different. For one thing, Paul was released from prison for a period of years and continued his ministry. Eventually, however, he was arrested again—this time under the authority of Emperor Nero, who hated Christians. This time Paul's prison was an infamous hole in which his meals were lowered down by use of a bucket. He did not receive visitors. And he was certain that he would soon be executed because of his faith.

It is with that backdrop that Paul sought to warn Timothy about the dangers Christians would face throughout this new phase in the life of the church. "But know this," Paul wrote, "that in the last days perilous times will come" (3:1).

The phrase "last days" is important. It refers to the age between the launch of the church and the Rapture of the church, which precedes the Tribulation. So, everything from the Day of Pentecost described in Acts 2 all the way up to the Rapture is encompassed in this phrase "the last days."

Importantly, Paul prophesied that this current age would be marked by "perilous times." The world would be a dangerous place—both physically and spiritually—for those who choose to follow Christ.

Paul was specific in his prophetic words. He identified nineteen separate characteristics that would define the "last days" and make them perilous—including that humanity would increasingly love themselves, love money, love pleasure, love wickedness, and attempt to incorporate religious worship without submitting to God's power.

Paul also prophesied that these nineteen characteristics would become more pronounced as we get closer to the end of this age. He wrote, "But evil men and impostors will grow worse and worse, deceiving and being deceived" (verse 13). As you may remember, this mirrors Jesus' prophetic announcement from the Olivet Discourse that the perils of our world will increase like a woman's labor pains—becoming more frequent and more intense until the moment of birth arrives (Matthew 24:4–8).

Let's consider what these prophecies mean for those of us living in these "last days."

REFLECT

1. What do you find most interesting or noteworthy as you read through 2 Timothy 3:1–15? Why?

2. Look again at the nineteen characteristics of "perilous times" in verses 1–5. Which of those characteristics seem most prominent in today's culture? (What are the top five, for example?)

3. Read 2 Thessalonians 2:1–12 to see another description of what life will be like as we approach the end of this age. Where do you see connections between that passage and 2 Timothy 3?

4. According to Jewish tradition, Jannes and Jambres (verse 8) were among Pharaoh's magicians who opposed Moses—and even entered Jewish society as secret agents to lead the people astray. How have you been impacted by false teachers or counterfeit beliefs in your spiritual life?

APPLY

5. Look again at 2 Timothy 3:10–15. What strategies did Paul recommend to Timothy for staying strong in the midst of these perilous times?

6. Of the nineteen characteristics that describe people during the "perilous times," which ones have some application to you? Which do you struggle with personally?

7. What are some ways you are currently being impacted by those negative aspects of our culture?

8. What are some specific steps you can take to grow and develop your character as a follower of Jesus?

AHEAD

Do you ever struggle with loving yourself more than you should? Do you feel the pull of money and all that it can buy in our culture? Do you have seasons when you are unthankful? Unloving? Unforgiving? What about headstrong?

In some ways, reading Paul's description of "perilous times" can feel more than a little convicting on a personal level. Perhaps even discouraging. Because even as disciples of Jesus, we are all moving through the process of sanctification. Each of us still deals with the reality of sin. We might wonder, *Am I the same as everyone else?*

My friend, don't give in to discouragement. As Paul told Timothy, "All who desire to live godly in Christ Jesus will suffer persecution" (verse 12). Worse, all of us will suffer failure. Yet even as we endure this process of sanctification, we can be confident in our justification—we can be confident that our sins were borne away on the cross and we are forgiven. Completely. We are righteous because Jesus is righteous. And we are on our way home.

All who desire to live godly in Christ Jesus will suffer persecution. But evil men and impostors will grow worse and worse, deceiving and being deceived.

2 TIMOTHY 3:12–13

Paul prophesied this current age would be marked by perilous times. The world would be a dangerous place, both physically and spiritually, for those who choose to follow Christ.

DAY 20

THE LORD IS NOT SLACK

But, beloved, do not forget this one thing, that with the Lord one day is as a thousand years, and a thousand years as one day. The Lord is not slack concerning His promise, as some count slackness, but is longsuffering toward us, not willing that any should perish but that all should come to repentance.

2 PETER 3:8–9

CONTEXT

The apostle Peter was nearing the end of his life, and he knew it. Like Paul, Peter was imprisoned in a dungeon in Rome because of his faith. He knew he was about to become one of the many Christians martyred at the whim of Emperor Nero, and he made that knowledge plain at the beginning of his second epistle to the church: "Yes, I think it is right, as long as I am in this tent, to stir you up by reminding you, knowing that shortly I must put off my tent, just as our Lord Jesus Christ showed me" (2 Peter 1:13–14).

That being the case, Peter wrote this final epistle almost as a last will and testament for the believers in the early church. He was offering his final thoughts, warnings, and encouragements before his death at the hands of a tyrant. And one of the main things Peter wanted to communicate in that final letter was a warning against false prophets in the church.

In chapter 3, Peter exhorted believers to be "mindful of the words which were spoken before by the holy prophets" (verse 2). Specifically, he wanted them to recall the many Old Testament prophecies that pointed forward to a future season of judgment, which we have labeled in these pages as the Day of the Lord.

Then Peter addressed the reality of false teachers: "Knowing this first: that scoffers will come in the last days, walking according to their own lusts, and saying, 'Where is the promise of His coming? For since the fathers fell asleep, all things continue as they were from the beginning of creation'" (verses 3–4).

It's fair to say that most of the early Christians believed Jesus would return soon. In fact, most expected the Rapture to occur within their own lifetimes—especially when they began to experience serious persecution at the hands of both Rome and the Jewish authorities. Then, as the years went by, false teachers began to proclaim that there would be no time of judgment. There would be no Day of the Lord and no return of Christ to punish evil and establish His kingdom. Everything would simply continue forward as it always had.

Peter rejected these teachings and exhorted those in the church to hold on to the truth spoken by the Old Testament prophets, spoken by Jesus Himself, and spoken by the apostles: that the day of judgment will come.

Peter also sought to help the church understand what seemed like a delay in God's imminent plan—namely, that God views time much differently, on a different scale, than we do as human beings (verse 8). And that what we might consider a "delay" in the return of Jesus is actually an extension of grace that allows more and more people the opportunity to receive salvation (verse 9).

Keep that background in mind as you work through the following questions.

REFLECT

1. Look at 2 Peter 3:1–9. How would you summarize the step-by-step arguments Peter made in those verses? What was the overall message he wanted to communicate?

2. Peter referenced the flood as an example of a previous time God judged the world (verses 5–6). Read Genesis 6:1–14 for more details on that event. What can we learn from that passage about God's nature and character? About judgment and grace?

3. The members of the early church believed that Jesus would return in their lifetimes, or at least "soon," yet almost two thousand years have passed. What does this delay reveal about God's nature and character?

4. Now take a look at 2 Peter 3:10–13. What can we learn from these verses about the future of our world? About the nature of God's judgment against evil?

APPLY

5. In his argument against false teaching, Peter referenced "words which were spoken before by the holy prophets" (verse 2). You have studied several prophecies in this study. Which ones have felt most meaningful or most powerful to you? Why?

6. We all have seasons or specific moments when we wish God would operate on our schedule rather than His own. When have you felt confused or frustrated because of what seemed like a delay on God's part? What happened next?

7. In what areas of life are you currently waiting for God to open a door on your behalf? What emotions are you experiencing during this time of waiting?

8. What specific steps can you take to affirm and demonstrate your trust in God even (or especially) during a season of waiting?

AHEAD

As we've seen, references to the Day of the Lord in Scripture typically point forward to the moment when Jesus returns to our world as King and physically, decisively carries out His wrath against the Antichrist, rebellious people, and the evil of humanity.

But there will come another day of God's wrath after that event—a second Day of the Lord. This event will take place at the end of the Millennium, which is the thousand-year period when Jesus reigns on earth as King. After those thousand years, Satan will be unleashed from the Abyss and will lead many people astray. There will even be another version of Armageddon in which humanity attempts to make war on God.

On that day, God will reforge our world. He will reforge heaven, as well. The result will be a new heaven and new earth, which Peter mentions in 2 Peter 3:13. We will discuss these events and these themes in greater detail as we move this study into the book of Revelation.

The Lord is not slack concerning His promise, as some count slackness, but is longsuffering toward us, not willing that any should perish but that all should come to repentance.

2 PETER 3:9

What we might consider a "delay" in the return of Jesus is actually an extension of grace that allows more and more people the opportunity to receive salvation.

DAY 21

THE TIME IS NEAR

*The Revelation of Jesus Christ, which God gave Him
to show His servants—things which must shortly take place.
And He sent and signified it by His angel to His servant John, who
bore witness to the word of God, and to the testimony of Jesus
Christ, to all things that he saw. Blessed is he who reads and those
who hear the words of this prophecy, and keep those things which
are written in it; for the time is near.*

REVELATION 1:1–3

CONTEXT

When the prophet Daniel was an old man and filled with sorrow about the state of Judah and Jerusalem, God sent an angel to offer a vision of the future. That vision covered seventy "weeks" of years—seventy periods of seven years each—that accurately predicted the unfolding of nations and empires over several hundred years. Those weeks were divided into sixty-nine weeks (483 years) between the proclamation to rebuild Jerusalem and the entrance of the Messiah into that same city, and then one final week that is yet to come—the seventieth week. When God's people rejected Jesus as their Messiah, the Father pressed pause on His plan for the Jewish people and pivoted toward the launch of the church.

Now that we arrive at the book of Revelation, we find the apostle John as an old man who is filled with sorrow about his separation from the churches he helped plant and lead for decades. By this time, every other member of the original twelve disciples had been martyred (save Judas, who committed suicide). John was still alive, but Rome had exiled him to the tiny island of Patmos to live out his final days in isolation.

There, in that sorrowful place, God gave John a vision that stretched far into the future—not just hundreds of years but thousands. Even into eternity. That vision contained many facets, which we will explore in the pages that follow. But one of the central themes is God's declaration of what will happen during the seventieth week of His plan for human history. Those seven years will be the most terrible and chaotic in human history, so much so that we typically refer to them as the Tribulation.

Now, it's common for people to believe that the primary theme of Revelation is the end of the world, or Armageddon, or the mark of the Beast, and so on. But that is not the case. The primary theme of Revelation is highlighted from the very first verse: "The Revelation of Jesus Christ, which God gave Him to show His servants—things which must shortly take place" (1:1).

The vision revealed to John is *primarily* concerned with Jesus Christ. This is *His* revelation. Specifically, while the church has mainly known Jesus as the Lamb of God who takes away the sin of the world, the book of Revelation introduces Him as King. *The* King. The One who will right all wrongs, establish justice, and reign on David's throne forever.

For that reason, Revelation is a book filled not with doom and gloom—but with hope. No matter how dark things become in our world, we can find hope in the knowledge that God is sovereign over history. He has a plan, and His plan is being unfolded according to His timing. In the end, the King will establish goodness, justice, and love in our world forever.

Let's start our exploration by focusing on Revelation 1:1–8.

REFLECT

1. Take a moment to read Revelation 1:1–8 out loud. As you do so, what catches your attention, or what do you find most interesting in those verses? Why?

2. Look again at verses 1–3. What can we learn from that passage about John's purpose for writing and distributing the book of Revelation?

3. Look back at Daniel 9:20–27 to see the "seventy weeks" prophecy supplied by the angel Gabriel. In your own words, how would you summarize the way that prophecy applied to Daniel's future and to our future?

4. Now look at John's vision of King Jesus in Revelation 1:9–20. What images do you find most striking in that vision? What do those images communicate?

APPLY

5. The beginning of any letter is an important way to set the tone for the rest of that correspondence. In your view, how does Revelation 1 set the tone for the rest of the book?

6. What emotions do you experience when you read John's description of Jesus in verses 9–20? What do you like best about that description, and why?

7. Jesus is the King of glory—the Alpha and the Omega. Our right response to Him is worship and praise. Whether in church or not, what does a typical experience of worshiping Jesus look like for you?

8. Where do you have an opportunity to add more expressions of worship and devotion to Jesus in your everyday life?

AHEAD

There was a long time when Revelation 1:7 caused a lot of consternation for readers of the Bible. Referring to Jesus, it says, "Behold, He is coming with clouds, and every eye will see Him, even they who pierced Him. And all the tribes of the earth will mourn because of Him. Even so, Amen."

Do you see the potential for trouble? Throughout the vast majority of human history, there was no way for "every eye" to see something at the same time. That's because we live on a sphere. If something is happening in the sky at one portion of the earth, it cannot be visible to a huge portion of the rest of the planet—it will be blocked out by the curvature of the earth.

In more modern decades, however, that problem has been solved. First by broadcast television and second by the internet. Now, we have no trouble conceiving a way for every person to lay eyes on Jesus when He returns in the clouds.

As always, Scripture is true. Sometimes we just have to wait for history to catch up before we can rightly understand that truth!

"I am the Alpha and the Omega, the Beginning and the End," says the Lord, "who is and who was and who is to come, the Almighty."

REVELATION 1:8

No matter how dark things become, we can find hope in the knowledge that God is sovereign over history. He has a plan, and His plan is being unfolded according to His timing.

DAY 22

A VISION OF THE THRONE

After these things I looked, and behold, a door standing open in heaven. And the first voice which I heard was like a trumpet speaking with me, saying, "Come up here, and I will show you things which must take place after this."

REVELATION 4:1

CONTEXT

We're used to thinking of Revelation as a book about the future, and that's true. But it's important to remember that John's vision started with Jesus offering a word to the churches of John's present day. Jesus gave specific messages to the churches in Ephesus, Smyrna, Pergamum, Thyatira, Sardis, Philadelphia, and Laodicea—seven congregations in a relatively close area of Asia Minor. Those messages contained both encouragement and warning. They all communicated the need to stand firm in the face of coming persecution.

Then, after those letters to the churches, the focus of John's vision moved from earth to heaven: "After these things I looked, and behold, a door standing open in heaven. And the first voice which I heard was like a trumpet speaking with me, saying, 'Come up here, and I will show you things which must take place after this'" (4:1).

Can you imagine standing on Patmos—a remote isle in the Aegean Sea encompassing only about thirteen square miles—and then seeing a door open in thin air to reveal . . . heaven? Heaven! More specifically, John saw a vision of a heavenly worship service in full swing.

This wasn't a generic worship service, either, but a prophetic glimpse of the future. When the Rapture takes place and all believers are gathered together as one family, all of heaven will erupt in praise. The angels, the cherubim, the seraphim, the principalities and powers and angelic forces in the heavenly realms, and the redeemed saints of all the ages will worship together, and that event is described for us in Revelation 4 and 5.

One of the critical images contained in those chapters is God's "throne." In fact, the book of Revelation as a whole is packed with references to God's throne. The importance isn't the chair itself but what it represents. Namely, God's throne is a symbol for His sovereignty—not just in heaven but in our world and throughout all creation.

The more we study the throne of God in the book of Revelation, the more we're reminded that while events on this earth may seem chaotic and meaningless, there is a King in the universe seated upon His throne, sovereign and in control. The throne represents authority and absolute power. In addition, John's vision in Revelation 4 reminds us of the necessity to worship our King for who He is and all that He has done. Yes, it's true that one of the purposes for that vision was to show John "things which must take place after this"—things that would take place after the Rapture. But it's no coincidence that everything began with worship.

Remember that as we work through the more "exciting" elements of John's vision in the book of Revelation. We're going to explore the Tribulation and the Antichrist and the cataclysms described by the seal judgments and bowl judgments and trumpet judgments. All of that is coming. But it begins with worship.

REFLECT

1. Look again at John's vision of heaven's throne room in Revelation 4:1–11. How would you summarize the emotional atmosphere of that vision? What feelings and themes carry through most strongly?

2. Like most prophetic visions—and especially those in Revelation—this passage is packed with imagery. Which images stand out to you as most interesting, and what do those images communicate?

3. The prophet Ezekiel received a similar vision back in Ezekiel 1:4–28. Where do you see similarities between those two visions? What do those visions communicate about God and heaven and the angels?

4. There are two songs recorded in Revelation 4: one in verse 8 and the other in verse 11. How do those songs contribute to your understanding of God?

APPLY

5. Revelation 4 is packed with worship. In your experience, what does it mean to worship God in a meaningful way? What does that look like for you?

6. When have you recently been in a situation or a setting that helped you experience God's glory? His majesty?

7. As is evident in Revelation 4, worshiping God goes beyond singing or attending church services. What are some practical steps you can take to add worshipful experiences to your everyday routine?

8. Jesus is King in heaven right now, which means He is sovereign over every situation right now—even the tribulations we face on earth. To what degree do you trust that God is watching over you? Explain your answer.

AHEAD

As mentioned earlier, John's peek through the doorway into heaven's throne room is a prophetic one. It points toward a moment in the future—likely the moment after the Rapture when all of heaven erupts in worship and praise because God has initiated the next phase of His plan for history.

However, that doesn't mean the references to God's sovereignty and authority and power are applicable only to the future. Certainly not! God is seated on His throne today. He is sovereign over the universe today. He has total control of His plan for history, which includes not only yesterday and tomorrow—but also today.

Therefore, you and I can be confident today. Because we know God is in control. More than that, we know from both Scripture and our own personal histories that God loves us, cares for us, and has gone to great lengths to secure us a future with Him.

Praise be to God for who He is and for all He has done!

Whenever the living creatures give glory and honor and thanks to Him who sits on the throne, who lives forever and ever, the twenty-four elders fall down before Him who sits on the throne and worship Him who lives forever and ever, and cast their crowns before the throne.

REVELATION 4:9–10

John's vision reminds us of the necessity to worship our King for who He is and all that He has done.

DAY 23

THE SEAL JUDGMENTS

I looked when He opened the sixth seal, and behold, there was a great earthquake; and the sun became black as sackcloth of hair, and the moon became like blood. . . . And the kings of the earth, the great men, the rich men, the commanders, the mighty men, every slave and every free man, hid themselves in the caves and in the rocks of the mountains, and said to the mountains and rocks, "Fall on us and hide us from the face of Him who sits on the throne and from the wrath of the Lamb! For the great day of His wrath has come, and who is able to stand?"

REVELATION 6:12, 15–17

CONTEXT

The book of Genesis describes a moment when Pharaoh, leader of one of the largest nations on earth, received a dream that predicted future events—seven years of plentiful harvest followed by seven years of devastating famine. Joseph interpreted that dream for Pharaoh, making sure to offer godly wisdom on how to deal with the coming crisis.

There are two ways to respond to Pharaoh's dream. One would be to ask, "How could God be so cruel as to allow seven years of famine across the known world?" The other way to respond would be, "What a wonderful gift that God warned the most powerful person on earth about a coming disaster so that many lives could be spared."

That same principle applies to the judgments that are prophesied throughout the book of Revelation. Those prophecies serve as warnings, alerting us to traumatic events coming in the future that we can either prepare for or avoid by following God's directives and depending on His providence. They provide all people with the opportunity to avoid disaster by embracing the gospel. Because remember: The Rapture removes believers from the earth *before* the Tribulation takes place.

The reality of the Tribulation and God's wrath and judgment against those who have rebelled against Him are the primary themes of Revelation 6–19. In reading those chapters, we encounter Jesus Christ poised to take back control of the earth. As the worthy Lamb, He comes to the throne and takes the scroll, which is the title deed to the earth.

As each of the seals of the scroll is broken, the scroll is unrolled to reveal multiple phases of God's wrath to be poured upon this wicked earth. By the time the seventh seal is broken, all the accumulated horrors of the entire Tribulation period have been unleashed. In the seventh seal we see the release of the seven trumpet judgments, and in the seventh trumpet judgment we see the unfolding of the seven bowl judgments. Each seal, each trumpet, and each bowl inflicts one terrible disaster after another with unrelenting regularity and intensity.

So how should we understand these terrible images, including those mentioned in Revelation 6:12–17? The answer is twofold.

First, God has promised throughout His Word that He will pour out His wrath against evil. He will pursue justice by punishing Satan and all who choose to follow him. We should not be surprised when those promises come true.

Second, we should be grateful that God has given us such extensive warnings about the judgment to come. Let's consider that perspective as we take a closer look at Revelation 6 and beyond.

REFLECT

1. Revelation 6:1–17 describes the pouring out of the "seal judgments" during the seven years of the Tribulation. How would you summarize the overall effect of those judgments? What will this period be like?

2. The first four seals (verses 1–7) unleash what are commonly called "the four horsemen of the Apocalypse." In terms of practical impact, what does each of these four riders represent?

3. The fifth seal judgment (verses 9–11) describes the cries of the martyrs throughout history who have been slain for their faith. What emotions are expressed in those verses? What emotions do you experience when you read them?

4. Take a moment to skim through the trumpet judgments (Revelation 8–9) and the bowl judgments (chapter 16). Which of the terrors and cataclysms listed in those chapters seem most terrifying to you? Why?

APPLY

5. The reality of God's future judgment is both horrifying and frightening—yet God has promised they will come to pass. In your mind, how do those judgments fit with God's nature and character as revealed through His Word?

6. The "four horsemen" described in Revelation 6 generally refer to the Antichrist, war, famine, and death. All of these will be increasingly prevalent during the Tribulation, but where do you see them impacting our world today?

7. What role does the church have in combating these destructive forces? Meaning, what (if anything) should we be doing about those four threats as we move toward the end of this age?

8. Followers of Jesus are exempt from God's judgment. Why, then, should we study and seek to understand these types of prophecies?

AHEAD

One of the criticisms often leveled at modern culture is that the wealthy and powerful often seem to be unaccountable for their actions. But of course such a reality has never been limited to modern culture. Throughout all culture and civilizations in human history, those who have wealth, influence, prestige, and power have taken advantage of those who were poor, needy, and anonymous—often without any notable consequences.

That will not be so when it comes to the judgment of God. Notice the emphasis during the sixth seal judgment: "And the kings of the earth, the great men, the rich men, the commanders, the mighty men, every slave and every free man, hid themselves in the caves and in the rocks of the mountains, and said to the mountains and rocks, 'Fall on us and hide us from the face of Him who sits on the throne and from the wrath of the Lamb! For the great day of His wrath has come, and who is able to stand?'" (Revelation 6:15–17).

There is no buying ourselves free from the judgment of God. There will be no craftily written laws that exclude those with political power. Not even those who are physically strong will be able to muscle their way out of the consequences of their evil actions.

God has promised to judge evil, and He will do so with terrible equity.

Now I saw when the Lamb opened one of the seals; and I heard one of the four living creatures saying with a voice like thunder, "Come and see."

REVELATION 6:1

God has promised throughout His Word that He will pour out His wrath against evil. He has given us extensive warnings about the judgment to come.

DAY 24

THE TWO WITNESSES

These are the two olive trees and the two lampstands standing before the God of the earth. And if anyone wants to harm them, fire proceeds from their mouth and devours their enemies. And if anyone wants to harm them, he must be killed in this manner. These have power to shut heaven, so that no rain falls in the days of their prophecy; and they have power over waters to turn them to blood, and to strike the earth with all plagues, as often as they desire.

REVELATION 11:4–6

CONTEXT

As we've established, the world will be a dark place during the Tribulation. Beyond all the chaos and cataclysms, one of the main reasons for that darkness will be the lack of saints, because all genuine believers will be removed at the Rapture. So, the world of the Tribulation will be a place of spiritual darkness unlike anything experienced in human history.

Still, there will be some light. Even during the Tribulation, God will not abandon the billions of people on the planet with no hope of salvation. Specifically, He will send two distinct sets of messengers who will proclaim the truth.

The first set of messengers are what Scripture calls the "two witnesses." Likely these witnesses will arrive immediately after the Rapture and begin to proclaim the truth of the gospel. They will also perform miracles and demonstrate supernatural power: "And if anyone wants to harm them, fire proceeds from their mouth and devours their enemies" (Revelation 11:5).

The message of these two witnesses will not be popular. They will warn that the disasters of the Tribulation are judgments the people have brought down upon themselves by rejecting Christ as Lord. They will accuse the people of turning Jerusalem, God's holy city, into a pit of depravity. They will refute the claims of the Antichrist and expose him for the Satan-controlled being he is. They will denounce the lie that man is innately good and improvable. They will warn of more judgments to come if the people do not turn from their gross depravity.

After the precise 1,260 days of their ministry, the two witnesses will be killed. Their bodies will lie in the streets, and the whole world will rejoice at their deaths—for a little while. After three days, the witnesses will be raised back to life and will ascend into heaven as a supernatural proof to the truth of their message.

The second set of messengers are the 144,000 Jewish evangelists described in Revelation 7:1–8 and 14:1–5. There will be twelve thousand evangelists from each of the twelve tribes of Israel, and they will sweep across the globe as witnesses for the truth of the gospel. While the servants of the Antichrist will receive the mark of the Beast (Revelation 13:18), these Jewish evangelists will be "sealed" by the Holy Spirit and protected throughout the Tribulation.

More than that, they will be incredibly effective. John writes, "After these things I looked, and behold, a great multitude which no one could number, of all nations, tribes, peoples, and tongues, standing before the throne and before the Lamb, clothed with white robes, with palm branches in their hands, and crying out with a loud voice, saying, 'Salvation belongs to our God who sits on the throne, and to the Lamb!'" (Revelation 7:9–10).

Yes, because of these witnesses, the Tribulation will be a time of spiritual revival from which a great multitude of saints will receive eternal life!

REFLECT

1. Look at Revelation 11:1–14, which describes the ministry of the "two witnesses." What can we say for certain about those witnesses based on that passage?

2. John's language in these verses is intentionally tied back to an earlier prophetic passage in Zechariah 4, especially verses 11–14. Where do you see similarities between those two passages? What can we learn about the two witnesses from Zechariah 4?

3. These two witnesses will have an extended ministry during the Tribulation, and they will be hated by the people. Where do you see authentic Christianity being rejected and despised by the world today?

4. Revelation 14:1–5 shows the fate of the 144,000 Jewish evangelists at the end of the Tribulation. What can we say for certain about their ministry and their reward based on these verses?

APPLY

5. Many Bible scholars have speculated that these two witnesses are Moses and Elijah. What evidence do you see in the text for that speculation?

6. Both the two witnesses and the 144,000 Jewish evangelists will be hated by those they are seeking to reach. How have you been exposed to the hatred our world feels for Christ and His kingdom?

7. When was the last time you had an opportunity to be a witness for Jesus—to tell someone about the gospel? How did you respond to that opportunity?

8. Where would you like to grow as a witness? Where would you like to become more skilled or more knowledgeable when it comes to evangelism?

AHEAD

As strange as it may seem, the Tribulation will be a time of unparalleled evangelism in our world. Even as Satan and the Antichrist attempt to assert control over the hearts and minds of all people, revival will break out. A great multitude will be saved. This is a wonderful prophetic truth!

Yet these realities should motivate us to spread the message of the gospel here and now, while we have the chance. Jesus told us, "Go therefore and make disciples of all the nations, baptizing them in the name of the Father and of the Son and of the Holy Spirit, teaching them to observe all things that I have commanded you; and lo, I am with you always, even to the end of the age" (Matthew 28:19–20).

When is "the end of the age"? Well, the Rapture is the transition from our current age, which in biblical terms is the "last days," and which others call the age of grace. The Rapture is the final moment of this age and the first moment of the Tribulation. Which means we still have time to obey Jesus' command!

Let's make it a priority *this very day* to spread the good news of salvation to all who need it.

"And I will give power to my two witnesses,
and they will prophesy one thousand two hundred
and sixty days, clothed in sackcloth."

REVELATION 11:3

Because of the two witnesses, the Tribulation will be
a time of spiritual revival from which a great multitude
of saints will receive eternal life.

DAY 25

THE ANTICHRIST

Then he opened his mouth in blasphemy against God, to blaspheme His name, His tabernacle, and those who dwell in heaven. It was granted to him to make war with the saints and to overcome them. And authority was given him over every tribe, tongue, and nation. All who dwell on the earth will worship him, whose names have not been written in the Book of Life of the Lamb slain from the foundation of the world.

REVELATION 13:6–8

CONTEXT

Since the life and ministry of Jesus Christ, there have been many powerful men who sought to conquer the world or remake it in their own image. Constantine. Genghis Khan. Napoleon Bonaparte. Adolf Hitler. All of those men are known for both their power and their cruelty. But all of them are mere foreshadowings of someone who claims the earth as his own during the Tribulation.

That person is the Antichrist.

As the apostle John wrote in one of his epistles, "Little children, it is the last hour; and as you have heard that the Antichrist is coming, even now many antichrists have come, by which we know that it is the last hour" (1 John 2:18). The Antichrist will be one of the primary symbols that mark the seven years of the Tribulation.

There are over one hundred passages of Scripture that describe the Antichrist, and yet the word *antichrist* itself is mentioned in only four verses in the New Testament—each time by the apostle John (1 John 2:18, 22; 4:3; 2 John 7). As the word suggests, the Antichrist is a person who is against Christ. The prefix *anti-* can also mean "instead of," and both meanings will apply to this coming world leader. He will overtly oppose Christ and at the same time pass himself off as Christ.

The Antichrist will aggressively live up to his terrible name. He will be Satan's superman who persecutes, tortures, and kills the people of God, making Hitler, Stalin, and Mao seem weak and tame by comparison.

More than twenty-five different titles are given to the Antichrist, all of which help paint a picture of the most despicable man who will ever walk the earth. He is a king with "fierce features, who understands sinister schemes" (Daniel 8:23). He is "the worthless shepherd" (Zechariah 11:17). He is "the man of sin" and "the son of perdition" (2 Thessalonians 2:3). And in Revelation 13, John calls him "the beast." Some scholars believe he is Satan incarnate. We know for certain that Satan gives him his power, his throne, and his authority.

We don't know who the Antichrist is, nor will we know before he seizes power. Scripture says he will rise up out of the sea (Revelation 13:1), which is a picture of an ordinary man stepping out from the "sea of humanity." But we do know what the Antichrist will accomplish: persecution, violence, murder, chaos, domination, blasphemy, deceit, and worship of himself. He will become everything Christ is not, and he will attempt to seize everything Christ is due.

If you feel hesitant to study such a horrific personage, I understand. Yet study is necessary so that we better understand the future of our world.

REFLECT

1. Revelation 13:1–10 uses a lot of imagery to introduce the Antichrist and his impact on the world. What are the primary images in those verses, and what do those images communicate?

2. What are some words you would use to describe the Antichrist based on that passage? What will he be like, and what will he do?

3. Daniel 7:1–8 contains a prophecy about the Antichrist—he is the fourth "beast" described in those verses. Where do you see similarities between that passage and Revelation 13? What can we learn about the Antichrist from Daniel 7?

4. The Antichrist will not be alone in his bid to conquer our world. Revelation 13:11–18 describes a second "beast," which is the false prophet who will aid the Antichrist in establishing a worldwide religion. What can we say for certain about the false prophet based on those verses?

APPLY

5. Both the Antichrist and the false prophet will be equipped and empowered by Satan, so that they form a sort of unholy trinity. Read Revelation 12:7–17. How do those verses add to your understanding of who Satan is and what he desires?

6. What are some systems, ideologies, or movements operating in today's world that you feel are especially anti (as in "against") Christ?

7. How have you seen the concept of the Antichrist elevated or even celebrated in popular culture?

8. In your opinion, is it a good use of time and energy for Christians to try to figure out who the Antichrist might be prior to the Rapture? Explain your reasoning.

AHEAD

Contemplating the Antichrist is a miserable business. So let's balance things out by spending some time contemplating Jesus, who is "the Christ"—the Anointed One.

First and foremost, Jesus is God. He is the Son, the second person of the Trinity, which means He has always existed and will always exist. He is eternal. He is all-powerful, all-knowing, and all-present. Everything that is true about God is true about Jesus. Which means Jesus is the source of all good in this world—love, joy, peace, laughter, beauty, and so much more.

Second, Jesus is our Savior. He joined our world by taking on flesh and being born of a virgin named Mary. He didn't come primarily to teach us or to set a good example. No, He came to save us. He willingly died on the cross so that His blood would provide forgiveness for all sin—if only we will receive it.

Finally, Jesus is our King. He exists now as King of the universe, but He will physically rejoin our world once more to reign as the rightful King promised so many times throughout Scripture. He is your King and mine. The King of kings and Lord of lords.

Then I stood on the sand of the sea. And I saw a beast rising up out of the sea, having seven heads and ten horns, and on his horns ten crowns, and on his heads a blasphemous name.

REVELATION 13:1

We don't know who the Antichrist is, nor will we know before he seizes power. But we do know what the Antichrist will accomplish: persecution, violence, murder, chaos, domination, blasphemy, deceit, and worship of himself.

DAY 26

THE FALL OF BABYLON

After these things I saw another angel coming down from heaven, having great authority, and the earth was illuminated with his glory. And he cried mightily with a loud voice, saying, "Babylon the great is fallen, is fallen, and has become a dwelling place of demons, a prison for every foul spirit, and a cage for every unclean and hated bird! For all the nations have drunk of the wine of the wrath of her fornication, the kings of the earth have committed fornication with her, and the merchants of the earth have become rich through the abundance of her luxury."

REVELATION 18:1–3

CONTEXT

It should come as no surprise that Jerusalem is the city most frequently mentioned in the Bible. But would you believe "Babylon" is next on the list? It's true. Scripture has more references to Babylon than any other city excepting Jerusalem.

Tellingly, those references are never positive. In terms of God's Word, the history of Babylon begins with the Tower of Babel in Genesis 11, which represents humanity's attempt to build a worldwide order that exists outside of God's power. That tower was a monument to rebellion against God, and things only got worse from there. The city became known as pagan, humanistic, and rebellious against God—unholy attributes permanently adhered to its name, making it perennially infamous.

The book of Revelation reveals that when the Antichrist seizes the reins of world government, his administration will be divided among three power centers. Rome will be his political base (Revelation 17), Jerusalem will be his control center for religion (2 Thessalonians 2:4), and Babylon will become his financial and economic hub (Revelation 18).

John lists twenty-eight commodities that will form the foundation of Babylon's worldwide commerce in the end times: "Merchandise of gold and silver, precious stones and pearls, fine linen and purple, silk and scarlet, every kind of citron wood, every kind of object of ivory, every kind of object of most precious wood, bronze, iron, and marble; and cinnamon and incense, fragrant oil and frankincense, wine and oil, fine flour and wheat, cattle and sheep, horses and chariots, and bodies and souls of men" (Revelation 18:12–13). Not only are these commodities still desired today, but they symbolize humanity's endless pursuit of material wealth. That pursuit will continue up to the moment of Christ's return.

In short, Babylon in the book of Revelation represents a unified financial system that covers our entire world. That system will be firmly in the control of the Antichrist, which means it will also be firmly in the control of Satan—and used for his purposes. It will become a new Tower of Babel. A new attempt to remake the world outside of God's power and authority.

For those reasons and more, God will bring about Babylon's destruction. And that destruction will be final: "Then a mighty angel took up a stone like a great millstone and threw it into the sea, saying, 'Thus with violence the great city Babylon shall be thrown down, and shall not be found anymore'" (verse 21).

When will this fall take place? At the end of the Tribulation. God will remove the loathsome work of the Antichrist and secular humanism, and in doing so He will clear the way for Christ to establish His kingdom on earth.

REFLECT

1. Revelation 17:1–18 describes Babylon as a "great harlot" represented by a woman riding on a beast. What are the key attributes of Babylon contained in those verses?

2. Look through Revelation 18:1–20 to see a broader picture of Babylon's fall. How do those verses add to your understanding of what Babylon represents and what it values?

3. Revelation 17 and 18 describe a future economic system established by the Antichrist, but the roots of that system are likely in place today. Where do you see similarities between John's descriptions of Babylon and our own culture?

4. Look specifically at Revelation 18:4–8. As followers of Jesus, what steps can we take to separate ourselves from the values and ungodly systems of our world?

APPLY

5. Throughout human history, many people have felt left behind by the world's financial systems, and those systems have certainly been used to cause harm. Where do you see our systems causing harm today?

6. In what ways do you feel pressure to conform to those systems—especially when it comes to business, money, and finances?

7. What role (if any) do you think Christians play in reforming those systems?

8. Even if the Antichrist and his financial systems are not operating today, Christians are called to stand out from the rest of the world. How are you obeying that call?

AHEAD

I think it's incredibly important that God specifically directed all who are saved to remove themselves from the "Babylon" of the Tribulation. John wrote, "And I heard another voice from heaven saying, 'Come out of her, my people, lest you share in her sins, and lest you receive of her plagues'" (18:4). In the same way, God calls us to get out of Babylon even now—that is, to separate ourselves from the godless spirit of the age, which is the spirit of Babylon that now permeates our culture.

I fear that today many believers are not heeding this call. They attempt to maintain dual citizenship in Jerusalem and Babylon, which Paul tells us is impossible: "For what fellowship has righteousness with lawlessness? And what communion has light with darkness? And what accord has Christ with Belial? Or what part has a believer with an unbeliever? And what agreement has the temple of God with idols? For you are the temple of the living God" (2 Corinthians 6:14–16).

As God's temple, we must keep a clean house for Him to occupy. We must sweep out the contaminations of self-love, worldly pleasure, and materialistic ambition. That doesn't mean rejecting money, but it does mean rejecting a system that values money above all else!

And on her forehead a name was written: MYSTERY, BABYLON THE GREAT, THE MOTHER OF HARLOTS AND OF THE ABOMINATIONS OF THE EARTH.

REVELATION 17:5

"Babylon" represents a unified financial system that will cover our entire world. It will become a new Tower of Babel—a new attempt to remake the world outside of God's power and authority.

DAY 27

ARMAGEDDON

Now I saw heaven opened, and behold, a white horse. And He who sat on him was called Faithful and True, and in righteousness He judges and makes war. His eyes were like a flame of fire, and on His head were many crowns. He had a name written that no one knew except Himself. He was clothed with a robe dipped in blood, and His name is called The Word of God.

REVELATION 19:11–13

CONTEXT

We've seen that the Antichrist and all of his forces will have many goals during the Tribulation period. They will set up a world government and attempt to seize power on every level imaginable. They will establish a worldwide economic system in order to control every financial resource. And they will require all citizens to worship the Antichrist (and, by extension, Satan) as part of a worldwide religion.

There's one more goal we have not yet discussed in detail: the destruction of Israel. The Antichrist will be intent on persecuting followers of Jesus, of course—although those will be in short supply near the beginning of the seven years. But one of Satan's primary goals as he seizes power will be to completely annihilate God's chosen people, the Jews.

Satan's first attempt at persecution will be the battle of Gog and Magog. This battle, which precedes the battle of Armageddon, will be a massive coalition of nations coming against Israel like swarms of hornets against a defenseless child, all of them led by a nation from the "far north," which may be Russia. Scripture tells us Satan will be the motivating force behind this invasion. But before he can accomplish his intended annihilation of Israel, she will be rescued by almighty God (Ezekiel 38–39).

Having failed to destroy Israel once, the Antichrist will gather all his forces together to deliver a final, crushing strike. However, by that point, the leaders of the nations will have seen the weak spots in the Antichrist's armor—they will have seen that he can be thwarted, which means he is not God. Therefore, they will attempt to break free from his rule. Huge armies will march against the Antichrist from the east, the south, and the north.

All these forces will converge near the plains of Mount Megiddo. Or, to use the Hebrew term, *Har Megiddo*. Armageddon. Humanity will be on the eve of a terrible battle right inside the borders of Israel—a battle for control of the world. Then, at the exact moment prepared since the foundations of the earth were laid, Jesus will return. The King will enter the scene. More than that, the King will enter the battle with all the forces of heaven behind Him:

> And I saw the beast, the kings of the earth, and their armies, gathered together to make war against Him who sat on the horse and against His army. Then the beast was captured, and with him the false prophet who worked signs in his presence, by which he deceived those who received the mark of the beast and those who worshiped his image. These two were cast alive into the lake of fire burning with brimstone. And the rest were killed with the sword which proceeded from the mouth of Him who sat on the horse. And all the birds were filled with their flesh (Revelation 19:19–21).

REFLECT

1. Revelation 19:1–10 set the stage for the battle of Armageddon by giving us another glimpse into heaven. How would you summarize the scene or the atmosphere described in those verses?

2. Look at the full scope of Armageddon as recorded in verses 11–21. What strikes you as most interesting or noteworthy about those verses? Why?

3. How do verses 11–21 add to your understanding of Jesus? What can they tell us about His nature, His character, and His mission in our world?

4. For those who have come to associate violence with evil, it can be hard to picture Jesus wielding a sword and striking down the armies of the Antichrist. What are some reasons why this battle will be necessary at the end of the Tribulation?

APPLY

5. Importantly, it is Jesus who conquers the armies of evil. He carries the authority to deliver judgment, while we do not. Still, what steps can followers of Jesus take to oppose the evil present in our world today?

6. Where do you currently have an opportunity to take one or more of those steps?

7. Look again at verse 10. Are there any areas of life in which you are in danger of worshiping something (or someone) other than God?

8. The reality of Armageddon reminds us to spread the gospel now, while we are still able to do so. Who among your friends and family members might be ready for a conversation about biblical prophecy? About Jesus?

AHEAD

When this current age ends, humanity will experience the terrible suffering of the Tribulation. And when the Tribulation ends, humanity will experience the horrendous violence of Armageddon. These are frightening realities, and they should rightly capture our attention.

The question before every single human being is critical: *Am I prepared?* Are you prepared for the end of this age? For the end of your life? For the end of human history?

I hope that is true for you, but I feel compelled to remind you that these topics go well beyond hope. We must be certain! And the only certain method of finding salvation and eternal life—of avoiding the Tribulation and Armageddon—is to place our trust in Jesus. He is the way, the truth, and the life. He is the only door to redemption.

If you are not certain of your security as a child of God, then take a moment to say this prayer right now:

Dear God, I admit I've sinned and fallen short of your glory. I realize the penalty for my sin is death, and I believe it was paid by the shed blood of Jesus Christ. I'm willing to repent of my sins, and I now confess Christ as my Savior and make Him the Lord of my life. In Jesus' name, Amen.

Pray it right this moment. Be certain today!

Now out of His mouth goes a sharp sword, that with it He should strike the nations. And He Himself will rule them with a rod of iron.

REVELATION 19:15

Humanity will be on the eve of a battle for the control of the world. Then, at the exact moment prepared since the foundations of the earth were laid, Jesus will return.

DAY 28

THE MILLENNIUM

Then I saw an angel coming down from heaven, having the key to the bottomless pit and a great chain in his hand. He laid hold of the dragon, that serpent of old, who is the Devil and Satan, and bound him for a thousand years; and he cast him into the bottomless pit, and shut him up, and set a seal on him, so that he should deceive the nations no more till the thousand years were finished. But after these things he must be released for a little while.

REVELATION 20:1–3

CONTEXT

The apostle Peter reminded us in his second epistle that "with the Lord one day is as a thousand years, and a thousand years as one day" (2 Peter 3:8). That being the case, there will be a wonderful "day" enjoyed by all of God's children after the chaos of the Tribulation and the terrors of Armageddon. That future period is called the Millennium.

Let's begin by taking the mystery out of the term *millennium*. It comes to us from a combination of the Latin words *mille*, which means "a thousand," and *annum*, which means "years." The word *millennium*, then, simply means "a thousand years." So, the Millennium is a literal period of one thousand years, which is scheduled for the future and will begin when Jesus comes again at the end of history to set up His earthly kingdom.

Importantly, this season of wonder and bliss will not take place in heaven. Meaning, we will not exist in an alternate dimension, nor will we be present in God's throne room in what we currently understand as heaven. Instead, the Millennium will take place right here on planet Earth. Once Jesus defeats the Antichrist and judges all those who rebelled against Him, He will remove Satan from the scene and establish His kingdom here with us. His throne will be in Jerusalem, and He will physically reign and be present with us for a thousand years.

As we've already seen in these pages, biblical prophecy is filled with predictions of a coming day when King Jesus will rule over the earth, with His saints as co-regents with Him. The first time, He came to redeem us, but the world rejected Him. When He comes the second time, He will come to rule in righteousness.

During this period, the great predictions of His earthly kingdom will be fulfilled. Kings will fall down before Him. Nations will serve Him. He will sit on the throne of David and establish His kingdom with justice and judgment. His people will be righteous, and Israel will inherit its land. War will be suspended, and the Lord's dominion will stretch from sea to sea.

In effect, the Millennium will be a "redo" of the garden of Eden on a huge scale. Unfortunately, the end result will be the same. After a thousand years, Satan will be released from the abyss. He will once again work to deceive the world—especially those who were born during the Millennium and did not experience life before Christ's reign. The Millennium will end with another rebellion against God, which will trigger a final end to our world but a new beginning for all who follow Christ.

REFLECT

1. Read Revelation 20:1–10 to see the entire scope of the Millennium. Based on those verses, what can we say for certain about that season of life?

2. Where do you see Satan's influence and work in our world today? What do you imagine life would be like if that influence and that work were to be removed?

3. Read Isaiah 11:1–10 to see an Old Testament prophecy about the Millennium. What specific promises did God make in those verses?

4. Also read Ezekiel 36:22–38 to get a sense of the prosperity God has promised His people during the Millennium. How does that passage add to your understanding of what we will experience during those thousand years?

APPLY

5. How do you respond to the idea of the Millennium? Do you feel more excited or confused about what you will experience during those thousand years? Why?

6. One of the key elements of the Millennium is that Christ will be King of all the earth. In what ways have you experienced dissatisfaction from human leaders in your lifetime?

7. The Millennium will be a season of great joy and abundance for all believers—including all believers from history. Which Christians are you most excited to meet and get to know during those thousand years?

8. Though the Millennium will be wonderful, it will not be heaven—especially given its end. What are some steps you can take now to prepare yourself for that future season of serving under the reign of Christ?

AHEAD

One of the more interesting features about life during the Millennium will be the extension of human life. This is actually a fascinating study in the Bible.

Before the flood of Noah's day, people lived to incredible ages. According to Genesis 5:27, Methuselah lived to be 969 years old. Some scientists believe the climate of earth was so different, the genetic pool was so young, and the grace of God was so fresh that people lived for many centuries. Many people believe the flood changed the nature of the earth, or perhaps a vapor canopy protected us from the ultraviolet rays of the sun and enhanced longevity. The climate of the world was the healthiest in history.

Of course, whatever sustained that climate did not last. Now, according to Psalm 90:10, our lifespan is about seventy or eighty years, give or take some. Despite the best efforts of our medical experts, there's little chance any of us will be a Methuselah.

But that will change in the Millennium, and human longevity will return to pre-flood levels. It's as though history will come full circle. Isaiah 65:20 says, "Never again will there be in it an infant who lives but a few days, or an old man who does not live out his years; the one who dies at a hundred will be thought a mere child; the one who fails to reach a hundred will be considered accursed" (NIV).

And I saw thrones, and they sat on them,
and judgment was committed to them.

REVELATION 20:4

Biblical prophecy is filled with predictions of a coming day when Jesus will rule over the earth—with His saints as co-regents with Him.

DAY 29

THE GREAT WHITE THRONE JUDGMENT

And I saw the dead, small and great, standing before God, and books were opened. And another book was opened, which is the Book of Life. And the dead were judged according to their works, by the things which were written in the books.

REVELATION 20:12

CONTEXT

It is a common and accepted notion in our world today that all people will be judged once their lives are over. But what does it mean to be "judged"? What does that process involve?

Most people in our culture would say that, at the end of our lives, God will judge each person by what he or she has done. Meaning, He will take a look at our lives individually, and He will look at each individual decision. During that process, He will count all the good things we did. He will count all the bad things we did—including the *really* bad things, such as murder, which have special weight. Then He will compare those two lists and make a decision about whether we are worthy of heaven.

That is what our culture deems to be a "fair" judgment. However, it is completely wrong when compared to what the Bible says about God's process for judging not only the world but also each individual human life.

According to God's Word, our eternal fate will be sealed at death, not by God weighing evidence after the fact. In the end times there will actually be two altogether separate judgments occurring at different times and being tried in different courts. The first is called the Judgment Seat of Christ; the second is the Great White Throne Judgment.

All authentic Christians will be judged in the first court, which will immediately follow the Rapture. "We must all appear before the judgment seat of Christ, that each one may receive the things done in the body, according to what he has done, whether good or bad" (2 Corinthians 5:10). The object of this court is not to determine guilt or to condemn because every person who passes through it will be a Christian. They are reprieved because grace covers their sins. In this court, believers' works will be evaluated to determine how they should be rewarded. (Think of this "judgment" like an Olympic judge who scores a performance.)

All unbelievers and pseudo-Christians will be judged in the second court, the Great White Throne Judgment: "Then I saw a great white throne and Him who sat on it, from whose face the earth and the heaven fled away" (Revelation 20:11). Individuals will not be graded on the curve system or evaluated by cultural opinions of right and wrong. They will be judged by the unbending standard of God's truth, and this judgment will be forever unalterable.

The only question that matters at the foot of this Great White Throne will be: "Is your name written in the Book of Life?" Meaning, have you received the gift of salvation that was provided for you by the death and resurrection of Christ? If the answer is no, then your fate will be sealed and your sentence final.

I know it's not fun to explore these themes, but it's critical. Eternity is at stake! So let's take a closer look at the prophetic promise of the Great White Throne Judgment.

REFLECT

1. If possible, read Revelation 20:11–15 out loud. What emotions do you feel when you read these verses? What questions come to mind?

2. Jesus offered a foreshadowing of this Great White Throne Judgment during His famous Sermon on the Mount. Read it in Matthew 7:13–23. Where do you see connections between those verses and Revelation 20?

3. In describing his vision of this future judgment, John emphasized the "lake of fire," which is a picture of eternal hell. Why is hell a necessary part of God's plan for eternity?

4. Death always involves a separation. When we die physically, our soul and spirit are separated from our body. How, then, should we understand the concept of a "second death"? What does that mean, and from what will a person be separated in that moment?

APPLY

5. Read 2 Corinthians 5:9–11 to learn more about the Judgment Seat of Christ. How do you respond to the promise that Jesus will review your life and potentially offer rewards for your service?

6. Followers of Jesus will not experience the Great White Throne Judgment because they are sealed by the blood of Christ. What steps do you typically take to express gratitude for your salvation?

7. The only question that matters is whether our names are written in the Book of Life. How would you answer that question?

8. There aren't many choices we make that are *final*. We generally have the option to redo, readjust, and recalibrate our decisions. Given this, what are some ways you can communicate the *finality* of this judgment to those who need to hear about it?

AHEAD

Here's an interesting question: When does eternal life begin? Most people would say after death. But then, as we've seen, many people don't take the Millennium into their calculations. So, does eternal life start after that thousand years? After the Great White Throne Judgment?

It's an interesting question. Thankfully, Jesus gave us a definitive answer: "Most assuredly, I say to you, he who hears My word and believes in Him who sent Me has everlasting life, and shall not come into judgment, but has passed from death into life" (John 5:24).

At the moment you hear the gospel message and believe—*that* is when you pass from death to life. That is when eternal life begins.

Therefore, if you are a believer in Jesus, you are experiencing eternal life *right now*! It's not something you have to wait for. It's not something that comes way at the back end of God's plan for humanity. Eternal life is yours in this very moment, so take it and take advantage of it in Jesus' name!

Then I saw a great white throne and Him who sat on it, from whose face the earth and the heaven fled away.

REVELATION 20:11

All unbelievers and pseudo-Christians will be judged in the second court, the Great White Throne Judgment. They will be judged by the unbending standard of God's truth, and this judgment will be forever unalterable.

DAY 30

ETERNITY

But I saw no temple in it, for the Lord God Almighty and the Lamb are its temple. The city had no need of the sun or of the moon to shine in it, for the glory of God illuminated it. The Lamb is its light. And the nations of those who are saved shall walk in its light, and the kings of the earth bring their glory and honor into it. Its gates shall not be shut at all by day (there shall be no night there). And they shall bring the glory and the honor of the nations into it. But there shall by no means enter it anything that defiles, or causes an abomination or a lie, but only those who are written in the Lamb's Book of Life.

REVELATION 21:22–27

CONTEXT

The very first sentence in the Bible establishes the creation of two things that have been vital to humanity ever since: "In the beginning God created the heavens and the earth" (Genesis 1:1). Everything that every human being has ever experienced has been confined to those two locations: heaven and earth.

Consider, then, this shocking verse that we find near the very end of God's Word: "Now I saw a new heaven and a new earth, for the first heaven and the first earth had passed away" (Revelation 21:1).

The word *new* in that verse is significant. The apostle John originally wrote the book of Revelation in the prevailing Greek language of his day, and there are two Greek words for "new." One of those words (*neos*) contained the idea of creating something from nothing—new in terms of time. The other word (*kainos*) suggested newness in terms of quality. It is this second word that John uses of the new creation at the end of the age—not utter destruction but utter transformation. God will take what He originally created and remake it or reforge it into something not just new but better.

The apostle Peter prophesied about this moment in startling detail: "But the day of the Lord will come as a thief in the night, in which the heavens will pass away with a great noise, and the elements will melt with fervent heat; both the earth and the works that are in it will be burned up" (2 Peter 3:10). The universe will pass through the smelt furnace of God's judgment and emerge in a pristine state, glorified, transformed, imperishable, and fitted for eternity.

When will this happen? After the Rapture of the church, the seven years of Tribulation, the battle of Armageddon, the return of Christ, the Millennium, and the Great White Throne Judgment. Once we've marked off each of the days on God's prophetic calendar, He will draw the curtains on human history, and the entire universe will undergo a purifying conflagration. All evidence of disease will be burned up. All evidence of disobedience will melt away. All the remnants and results of sin, sorrow, and suffering will be destroyed.

Then, out of the smoldering ruins, God will re-create all physical reality, and He will bring forth a fresh universe—a new heaven and a new earth.

Next, you might be wondering what that new heaven and earth will be like. What will we experience in that reality? What will we do? What will we be like ourselves? These are important questions, so let's take a deeper look at God's Word in Revelation 21 and 22.

REFLECT

1. Start your exploration of the eternal state by reading Revelation 21:1–26. What specific promises are contained in that chapter? Which of those promises feels most exciting to you, and why?

2. Verse 3 describes God dwelling with His people and says, "God Himself will be with them and be their God." In your life right now, what helps you draw closer to God? In what circumstances do you feel closest to Him?

3. The city called "New Jerusalem" will be the crown jewel of the new heavens and new earth in the eternal state. It will be the capital city of the new earth. What can we say for certain about that city based on verses 9–21?

4. Revelation 22:1–5 offers another glimpse at what life will be like in our eternal state. What specific promises did God give to us in those verses?

APPLY

5. We rightly think of heaven as God's dwelling place, which means heaven can tell us a lot about God Himself. How do the passages we've studied above add to your understanding of God's nature and character? His values?

6. What emotions do you experience when you read Revelation 21 and 22? Why?

7. Which of God's promises about heaven feels the weightiest in your life right now? Which of those promises seems most important?

8. What have you enjoyed most about this study of biblical prophecy? Why?

AHEAD

As we wrap up this study together, I want to remind you of one important truth: Biblical prophecies are God's promises to humanity.

In these pages, we have studied thirty of the most important prophetic passages in the Bible, and those passages have revealed what will happen in human history. Not what *might* happen, but what *will* happen. The texts we have read are not suggestions. They are not educated guesses. They are not possibilities based on statistical analysis.

No, we have been studying God's prophetic promises. Of course, many of those prophecies have already been fulfilled, which builds our faith. But there are many promises yet to be fulfilled—including the Rapture, the Tribulation, the second coming of Christ, the establishment of the Millennium, the Great White Throne Judgment, and the re-creation of our universe into a new heaven and new earth.

Those promises will come to pass because they come from God. Believe it! Build your life around those promises, and look forward with great anticipation to all that is in store.

Now I saw a new heaven and a new earth, for the first heaven and the first earth had passed away.

REVELATION 21:1

Out of the smoldering ruins, God will re-create all physical reality, and He will bring forth a fresh universe—a new heaven and a new earth.

ABOUT DR. DAVID JEREMIAH AND TURNING POINT

Dr. David Jeremiah is the founder of Turning Point, a ministry committed to providing Christians with sound Bible teaching relevant to today's changing times through radio and television broadcasts, audio series, books, and live events. Dr. Jeremiah's common-sense teaching on topics such as family, prayer, worship, angels, and biblical prophecy forms the foundation of Turning Point.

David and his wife, Donna, reside in El Cajon, California, where he serves as the senior pastor of Shadow Mountain Community Church. David and Donna have four children, twelve grandchildren, and one great-grandchild.

In 1982, Dr. Jeremiah brought the same solid teaching to San Diego television that he shares weekly with his congregation. Shortly thereafter, Turning Point expanded its ministry to radio. Dr. Jeremiah's inspiring messages can now be heard worldwide on radio, television, and the internet.

Because Dr. Jeremiah desires to know his listening audience, he travels nationwide holding ministry events that touch the hearts and lives of many people. According to Dr. Jeremiah, "At some point in time, everyone reaches a turning point; and for every person, that moment is unique, an experience to hold on to forever. There's so much changing in today's world that sometimes it's difficult to choose the right path. Turning Point offers people an understanding of God's Word as well as the opportunity to make a difference in their lives."

Dr. Jeremiah has authored numerous books, including *Escape the Coming Night* (Revelation), *The Handwriting on the Wall* (Daniel), *Agents of the Apocalypse*, *Agents of Babylon*, *A Life Beyond Amazing*, *Overcomer*, *Everything You Need*, *Forward*, *The Jesus You May Not Know*, *The God You May Not Know*, *Where Do We Go From Here?*, *The World of the End*, *The Great Disappearance*, and *The Coming Golden Age*.

stay connected to the teaching of

DR. DAVID JEREMIAH

• • • • • • • • •

Publishing | Radio | Television | Online

From the Publisher

GREAT STUDIES

ARE EVEN BETTER WHEN THEY'RE SHARED!

Help others find this study:

- Post a review at your favorite online bookseller.
- Post a picture on a social media account and share why you enjoyed it.
- Send a note to a friend who would also love it—or, better yet, go through it with them!

Thanks for helping others grow their faith!